DR. RONNIE W. FLOYD

It's Dividing
The Family,
The Church,

And a Nation

THE GAY AGENDA

New Leaf Press

First printing: June 2004

ISBN: 0-89221-582-8
Library of Congress Number: 2004106647

Printed in the United States of America

Please visit our website for other great titles:

www.newleafpress.net

For information regarding author interviews,
please contact the publicity department at (870) 438-5288.

MY SINCERE DEDICATION . . .

of this book is to my church,

the First Baptist Church of Springdale

and the Church at Pinnacle Hills in Rogers,

Arkansas, for their unwavering commitment to God's

Word, the Bible, and their loving support to their senior

pastor, yours truly, as I have the privilege to proclaim

it as the Only Truth for today. In partnership,

we proclaim it to northwest Arkansas,

America, and the world.

I GIVE THANKS . . .

To New Leaf Press for its willingness to publish and turn around this project in jet speed. As soon as the idea was shared and discussed, they embraced it quickly. They have done what few other publishing companies would have been willing to do . . . throw out the normal rules of timelines and do a project that is needed in our country. Thanks to all the faithful workers at New Leaf Press and for paying the price to help get this needed word out to the world.

In my new relationship with this company, it has been a joy to work with Tim Dudley, president. He has become a friend, an encourager, and a partner in sharing words of assistance to all those who want to hear. Thanks, Tim, for all you have done for me and the success of this project.

I give thanks to my writing friend, Jim Fletcher, of New Leaf Press. He has provided me with outstanding assistance in this project, adding so much to it. So Jim, you know all you have done and thanks so much for everything. Your spirit of cooperation was refreshing.

I am also thankful to Laura Welch for her work in the publicity area. She has been wonderful to work with us, especially her work with my assistants here.

Those assistants who have helped along the way are Gayla Oldham, Melissa Swain, Becky Fletcher, and Delores Breeding. They are always encouragers in my life. Additionally, my young summer assistant of 2003, Chris Johnson, provided me with some initial research that launched this burden God had given to me.

So many other people in our organization assisted in areas of television and providing materials for publicity . . . you know who you are and I say thanks.

I also thank my great wife, Jeana, for her willingness to let me work at nights on projects such as these. As well, for the willingness to stand courageously with me on a project like this, realizing it might eventually alter a few things we do along the way.

Finally, to my dear Lord Jesus Christ, I say thanks. Thanks for Your words of life given to us in the Bible . . . our authority for life. We join Him in the effort of upholding genuine family in this nation and world.

CONTENTS

DEEPENING DIVISIONS

The scene on my television astonished me.

During one episode of a popular primetime drama, the "president" of the United States berated a woman portraying a conservative talk show host. He had taken exception to her views on homosexuality. My eyes widened as his anger rose.

"I like your show. I like how you call homosexuality an abomination," he said sarcastically.

"I don't say homosexuality is an abomination, Mr. President," she replied. "The Bible does."

"Yes, it does!" he shouted. "Leviticus 18:22." He was just warming up. "I wanted to ask you a couple of questions while I had you here. I'm interested in selling my youngest daughter into slavery as sanctioned in Exodus 21:7. She's a Georgetown sophomore, speaks fluent Italian, always cleared the table when it was her turn. What would a good price for her be?"

Their eyes locked and he continued: "While thinking about that, can I ask another? My chief of staff, Leo McGarry, insists on working on the Sabbath. Exodus 35:2 clearly says he should be put to death. Am I morally obligated to kill him myself or is it okay to call the police?" The radio host shifted uncomfortably. "Here's one that's really important, 'cause we've got a lot of sports fans in this town. Touching the skin of a dead pig makes one unclean, Leviticus 11:7. If they promise to wear gloves, can the Washington Redskins still play football? Can Notre Dame? Can West Point?"

The scene ended with the host humiliated and the president proudly defiant. He had taken a stand for an aggressively promoted but biblically condemned lifestyle. His barrage of questions had left his speechless opponent looking foolish. More than that, it cleverly advanced an agenda that increasingly has me worried.

Far beyond a single scene on one television program, a much more pervasive problem covers our land like a dark cloud. It seems that everything you see these days, everything you read, and everything you hear, is about the gay lifestyle.

This issue is dividing homes, churches, and an entire nation. Families are devastated. Church denominations are being ripped apart. Protestors rage at each other across picket lines. These divisions cause untold grief.

I hope you are aware that what once was whispered in the shadows now roars like a lion, as brazen and threatening as anything our culture has ever seen. I do not speak of a skirmish or a conflict or a disagreement here; I speak of a war. The proponents of the gay lifestyle have declared war against our culture, and they have an agenda. Charles Colson has said regarding the fight over same-sex marriage, "The Mother of all battles in the culture. Today people want personal autonomy and sexual freedom."[1] We need to be aware of it and to be prepared to make a decision regarding it.

The television program dialogue quoted above illustrates the goal of this sophisticated agenda: the effort to gain not just tolerance, but acceptance, and even celebration, of the gay lifestyle.

I agonize over the culture war raging across our land. Shrill and counter-productive voices on both sides of the divide demand to be heard. And in the midst of all the shouting, liberal causes have made great strides.

Gay marriages and same-sex ceremonies seem to have bloomed suddenly across the length and breadth of the country — but the forces preparing the ground have been at work for a very long time.

John Shelby Spong, the infamous and happily radical Episcopal bishop, has long advocated gay rights. In his autobiography, *Here I Stand*, Spong alludes to a scholar who mentored him as a young seminary student at North Carolina. This scholar had postulated that the apostle Paul had been a repressed gay man; hence, the reformed Pharisee's railings against homosexuality!

Spong has no way of knowing, of course, that Paul was homosexual or not. Yet this fact doesn't deter him in the least from making the gross assertion. When you read his works, it quickly becomes clear that he reached his conclusions, not through careful biblical study, *but via his feelings and political leanings*. No doubt he feels genuine compassion for the ostracized of our society. At least on that point, I'm there with him.

But we part company when he leaps to a radical re-thinking of traditional family and marriage. He demonstrates that the goals of a few threaten the freedom of many in America today.

Unprecedented events occurring in our nation and shameful episodes taking place in the courts and churches of our land have caused me to speak out about the Gay Agenda. I speak out of brokenness, bearing in mind the many families who have lost precious ones to the gay lifestyle. Only a person who has no love in his heart would fail to be moved by the horrific stories of suffering and dying AIDS patients. Social

> *The goals of a few threaten the freedom of many in America today.*

isolation and loneliness is another common aspect of this lifestyle — and the unhappiness and misery of its deceived adherents make me sick at heart.

It saddens me to see fathers and sons separated because of homosexuality. A young man "comes out" and the resulting years of silence destroy what once was a vital relationship. I grieve when a mother simply stops mentioning what's happening in the life of her lesbian daughter.

The divisions are deepening in our families.

Those pushing the Gay Agenda do not have the right to impose their chosen lifestyle on the rest of society. If left unopposed, their efforts to mainstream the lifestyle will annihilate the family as we know it.

I feel a great burden to issue a warning to proponents of traditional marriage: the Gay Agenda is dividing families. It is dividing an entire nation. And it is beginning to win some major battles.

The courts are deluged with same-sex cases. Politicians stagger all over the map, uncertain where to stand. Students, moved by compassion and tolerance, are asking their parents just why the gay lifestyle is incompatible with the concept of healthy, traditional families.

In the Christian community, the dividing lines feel especially painful. The Gay Agenda is now making major advances into the Church. According to *USA Today*, five of the major denominations in America are openly ordaining gay clergy and blessing same-sex unions.

Recent episodes at the annual meeting of the Episcopal Church have especially ignited this issue. When the Rev. V.

Gene Robinson, an openly gay clergyman, was elected as bishop of the Diocese of New Hampshire, both rejoicing and lamentation broke out in that denomination as never before.

In March 2004, a United Methodist Church court charged an openly gay minister with violating the denomination's *Book of Discipline*, which states clearly that homosexuality is at odds with the Bible. The jury acquitted her, claiming a lack of compelling evidence!

The divisions are deepening among Christians.

Imagine the surprise (okay, outrage!) of a mom and dad in North Carolina who recently saw an egregious example of what passes for the education of their first-grade daughter. Michael and Tonya Hartsell "couldn't believe it" when they read about Prince Bertie, a character in the book *King & King*, who from a group of eligible marriage partners chooses . . . Prince Lee! The Hartsells complained, but received only a lukewarm response from school officials, who said that the book had been on library shelves for more than a year. "What might be inappropriate for one family, in another family is a totally acceptable thing," said the school's principal, Elizabeth Miars.

The divisions are deepening in our schools.

Parents, be warned: in our culture, moral relativism is king. "Truth" is whatever one wishes it to be. As a result, your children have become vulnerable to world views that can do them great harm.

The strategy everywhere in our culture is to get you to see the gay lifestyle or gay couples as no different from anyone else. The agenda is also trying to desensitize you to their verbiage and their lifestyle. In other words, *If you get used to us, you will eventually ignore us or accept us.* The bombardment is working; a great deal of the desired desensitization already has occurred. Meanwhile, the gay lobby continues to sing its theme song of inclusiveness.

The Gay Agenda is finding a place throughout our schools, textbooks, and media, straight into the hearts of children and young people. Beware, administrators, teachers, students, and parents! The gay lifestyle is being actively promoted in books, by speakers, in seminar themes . . . in fact, it's everywhere. And struggling to figure it all out is that oldest of human institutions, the family.

Make no mistake, two irreconcilable agendas are at war.

Where do you stand in this great divide?

Chapter 1

A MARRIAGE OF TRUTH AND LOVE

T he German port city of Lubeck, like so many European towns, boasts an exquisite beauty. The waters of the Baltic Sea lap its shores, and in springtime flowers paint tree-lined boulevards. Young and old enjoy the cultural richness.

If you could transport yourself back to the 1930s, however, you wouldn't see such an idyllic Lubeck. Hitler's national socialism had filled the city with ugliness, like vast fields of diseased crops blighting the town. Nazi ideology affected all aspects of life. Into this gloom walked Friedrich-Paul von Groszheim, a young gay man.

In 1937, police arrested von Groszheim, along with 230 other men. A year later, he was arrested again. This time, torture preceded an ultimatum: life in a concentration camp, or castration.

Staring at "life" in a camp, von Groszheim chose castration. He survived the war and told his story only in 1992. He described how an unknown number of homosexuals were arrested in Nazi Germany, where laws enacted by Hitler's courts condemned this minority population to prison. Once released, they found post-war conditions not much better:

> The 1935 version of Paragraph 175 [from an ear-lier part of the 1871 Criminal Code, now targeting homosexuals] remained in effect in the Federal Re-public [West Germany] until 1969, so that well after liberation, homosexuals continued to fear arrest and incarceration.[1]

In fact, homosexuals often have been singled out for persecution. Such harassment has come from many sources: the Nazis, secular groups, even from within the Church. The 1998 beating death of Matthew Shepard, a gay university student in Wyoming, illustrates that such deadly hatred can rise up in our country just as easily as it did in 1930s Germany. As Matthew's mother, Judy, outlined in a *USA Today* column, violence against gays has not abated since her son's death:

- Sakia Gunn, a teenage lesbian, was stabbed to death in New Jersey in 2003.

- F.C. Martinez, another teenager ("transgender"), was murdered in 2001.

- In Hayward, California, prosecutors are preparing a case against three young men who beat and strangled another "transgender" teen, going so far as to describe the crime as an execution. Eddie Araujo, 17, was murdered in 2002 after having sex with two of the accused killers. They became enraged over the apparent deception used by Araujo, and confronted the youth one night. After being choked, hit with a skillet, punched in the face, tied up, and strangled, Araujo was buried in a shallow grave near Lake Tahoe.[2]

Godless hatred of homosexuals does not always lead to murder, of course. In Kansas, well-known pastor Fred Phelps, a militant opponent of gays, Jews, blacks, and other minorities, is a local celebrity. He travels the country, staging protests of gays and lesbians. Phelps has gone so far as to erect an offensive "monument" to Matthew Shepard, in a local Wyoming park. And Phelps has his allies. Recently I opened my paper to see an article about same-sex controversies. The story featured a photograph showing hate-filled protestors holding a sign that read, "Homosexuals Are Possessed by Demons."

This kind of loveless tactic does nothing positive. It only reinforces stereotypes of Christians as hateful bigots.

By now, I suppose you may be asking yourself, *Why mention these sorry episodes at the beginning of a book on the Gay Agenda?* I recount them because in our staunch opposition to sin, we must take care never to cross the line into hatred of the sinner — and as sinners ourselves, that's often easier said than done.

And yet it must be said.

So, before we go any further, let's remind ourselves of one clear and unalterable fact: the Bible gives absolutely *no* sanction to homo-sexuality. None. Never does God approve of it. Never does He endorse it. Never does He smile at it.

> In our staunch opposition to sin, we must take care never to cross the line into hatred of the sinner.

Nevertheless, God loves the Friedrich-Pauls and Matthew Shepards of this world. He loves all of us, even though all of us are broken and sinful.

INTO HOT WATER

I firmly believe it is possible to stand on God's truth at the same time that we love broken and sinful people. I believe there is a way to practice that which God wants us to practice. I believe, in other words, that there is a way we can love the sinner even as we oppose the sin.

Would you believe that such a conviction has gotten me into hot water with a lot of angry folks? These days, I find myself in the odd position of being attacked by both the right and the left.

On the left, secularists and liberals take exception to my clear opposition to the gay lifestyle. They tend to ignore the assistance that my church and I provide for gay individuals and their families.

On the right, some interpret any ministry to those involved in the gay lifestyle as "liberal" and "compromising." But I never apologize for our stance that practicing homosexuals can attend our church; in fact, I pray that they will, because in time I believe the Holy Spirit of God will convict them of their sin, they will see the need to change, and God's grace *will* transform them.

I believe the gay issue really comes down to the nature of truth and love. I don't see how we can win without equally embracing both. If we serve a Savior "full of grace and truth" (John 1:14), then how can we opt for one over the other? God does not call us to speak the truth without love, but to speak the truth in love (Eph. 4:15).

I maintain that the two must go hand in hand. But before that can happen, we first have to understand what we're talking about.

WHAT IS LOVE?

If you could count the number of grains of sand on a beach, you could count the number of definitions for love.

The entertainment industry presents "love" as adultery, lust, and sexual perversion. A sports enthusiast "loves" a particular athletic event or league. We "love" certain foods. And the definitions continue.

In a 2001 issue of *Open Hands: Shaping an Inclusive Church*, the Rev. Chip Aldridge invited young people to "claim and name"[3] their sexual preference. Among the questions he asked: "How can you really know if you're gay?" and "Can you still be a Christian if you are queer?"

Aldridge, director of admissions at Wesley Theological Seminary in Washington D.C., is an ordained United Methodist minister. The theme of the *Open Hands* article is God's love. Aldridge claimed, "God loves us queer folk, too!"

So much for Aldridge's view of what love is; the Bible has a very different take on it. An often-overlooked passage from God's Word tells us exactly what true love is:

> And this is love: that we walk in obedience to his commands (2 John 6).

Jesus said the very same thing: "If you love me, you will obey what I command. . . . Whoever has my commands and obeys them, he is the one who loves me. . . . If anyone loves me, he will obey my teaching. My Father will love him, and we will come to him and make our home with him. He who does not love me will not obey my teaching" (John 14:15–24).

Both of these New Testament descriptions of "true love" line up with the picture given in the Old Testament: "And now, O Israel, what does the LORD your God ask of you but to fear the LORD your God, to walk in all his ways, to love him, to serve the

LORD your God with all your heart and with all your soul, and to observe the LORD's commands and decrees that I am giving you today for your own good?" (Deut. 10:12-13).

Make sure you don't miss the amazing claim God makes in that last passage. Why does God tell us what to do? Why does He give us His instructions? He gives us His "commands and decrees" *for our own good*. That's what true love does; it wants only the best for the beloved.

Do we need to recall what happens to people when they don't follow God's commands? Did the Israelites know what real love was when they started worshiping the golden calf in the wilderness? Did young German men know what real love was when they fell under the spell of Hitler and began slaughtering defenseless men, women, and children? Do Hollywood actors know what real love is when they live or promote a gay lifestyle?

Because God loves us, He delights to walk into the lives of young girls who have determined that they are of a lesbian lifestyle. He loves to walk into the life of a young boy who determines that he is of a gay lifestyle. He loves to walk in when sociologists say that homosexuality is normal and that the world and the culture has accepted it. God loves to walk in and turn things around. He loves to do what looks humanly impossible. He loves to do what is best for us — and that includes directing us away from a homosexual lifestyle.

Do you know the main reason why the gay community is growing? It's growing because children and students want to be accepted

God loves to walk in and turn things around. He loves to do what looks humanly impossible.

and *loved*. All of us hunger for love. We want to feel valued. We want to feel cherished. And I think God's church has a lot of room for improvement in this area. We have a lot to learn about how to love those we may find unlovable.

What is love? I believe that to answer the question accurately, we must tie it to another famous query, from Pilate to Jesus: "What is truth?"

WHAT IS TRUTH?

Former Senator Bob Dole is known for his dry humor. When he's asked to comment on an issue, often he'll answer with a laconic, "Whatever." Now, I don't think Dole is *that* uninterested; he's just trying to get a laugh. But such a *whatever* attitude well describes the post-modern mindset of this country. And it's dangerous.

Postmodernism has been described as a room without walls, floor, and ceiling. It has no boundaries, no limitations — anything goes. Such a "whatever" mindset says, "You have your truth, I have mine. You believe what you want to believe, I'll believe what I want to believe." In other words, there is no absolute truth. And that means that truth is up for grabs.

The Rev. Barbara Cawthorne Crafton, a liberal Episcopalian pastor, says she is certain that the Bible is not the source of absolute truth. Her 1996 sermon, "Can You Believe It?" is all about the human inability to find truth. As odd as it may sound, she says she is certain that truth is not certain.

Her sermon outlines several reasons why she believes we cannot rely on God's Word as an infallible record of real history and real truth. Following this thinking to its logical conclusion, she insists:

> Whether you're attempting to discern the spiritual discipline appropriate for you or to discern your moral judgment of a sexual act, you're not going to be able to "follow the Bible" to the letter. Even people who think they do, they don't. It's not going to provide you with answers without your having to use your head. And, since most of us respect our own judgment and want to use it as best we can, this is just as well. To a great degree, we are on our own in making ethical decisions, in evaluating our histories, in comprehending the meaning of them. We will not find easy-to-follow recipes for our behavior in Scripture. Our primary tool is our own intelligence.[4]

Is this really how we are to determine the right path to follow? A creed based on feelings or on limited human intellect?

God forbid. I know that one day I might "feel like" following a radically different course than I "feel like" another day.

No biblical Christian can accept a definition of truth that relies on changing feelings or on the human ability to decide what is right and wrong. The Bible tells us that God "does not change like shifting shadows" (James 1:17) and that the Lord remains forever the same; in fact, that is why we can trust that He will never change his mind about saving us (Heb. 1:11; Mal. 3:6). Because the words God speaks reflect His character, they also do not change and will last forever (Isa. 40:8; 1 Pet. 1:25).

This explains why Jesus could say, "Do not think that I have come to abolish the Law or the Prophets; I have not come to abolish them but to fulfill them. I tell you the truth, until heaven and earth disappear, not the smallest letter, not the least stroke of a pen, will by any means disappear from the Law until everything is accomplished." And that explains why He could add, most appropriately for these difficult days, "Anyone who breaks one of the least of these commandments and teaches others to do the same will be called least in the kingdom of heaven, but whoever practices and teaches these commands will be called great in the kingdom of heaven" (Matt. 5:17–19).

As with every other aspect of life, if we follow scriptural guidelines, we will follow the path of truth. We'll know how to treat others. We'll know what ethics are. We'll know what true love is (and not what Britney Spears or Madonna tell us it is).

While many choose the gay lifestyle today because it "feels right," God has outlined very clearly how we are to view this lifestyle:

> Don't you realize that this is not the way to live? Unjust people who don't care about God will not be joining in his kingdom. Those who use and abuse each other, use and abuse sex, use and abuse the earth and everything in it, don't qualify as citizens in God's kingdom. A number of you know from experience what I'm talking about, for not so long ago you were on that list. Since then, you've been cleaned up, given a fresh start by Jesus, our Master, our Messiah, and by our God present in us, the Spirit (1 Cor. 6; MSG).

Anyone who does not believe that the Bible is God's Word is like the person who tries to live in a room with no walls, floor, or ceiling. Those who embrace the gay lifestyle feel the dread and fear that comes from living without a moral anchor. Floating about in space is

Those who embrace the gay lifestyle feel the dread that comes from living without a moral anchor.

not the most secure place to be. For some, the gay lifestyle really does seem like free-fall, and it terrifies them. Contrary to Ms.

Cawthorne Crafton, I'm quite certain that I am not speaking truth if I leave a gay person in such a terrifying position.

Of course, my critics on the left repeatedly tell me that I am divisive because of my stance on homosexuality; they urge me to "be more loving." But I am completely unwilling to abandon the truth. I am not willing to separate a sinner from his God, who can save. This is in stark contrast to the Rev. Cawthorne Crafton:

> What we do not have is certainty. Is there a way I can know beyond doubt that my actions are in accordance with the will of God? Will I find respite from the uncertainties of modern life in the pages of this holy book? Can I fully understand what the truth is and know beyond doubt that I am not in error? No. All I can do is try, knowing before I begin that my effort will be less than perfect. That I won't get it all just right. And being gentle enough on myself, and humble enough before others, to accept my limitations. I can never be absolutely sure, but I still must try to understand, because one of the things that makes me a human being is trying to understand.[5]

How can we then be sure of anything? How can we know what truth is?

Syndicated columnist Charles Krauthammer, writing in *Time*, indicated that he understands where post-modern thought

— elastic truth — can take us. In a piece about same-sex unions, he says:

> In other words, if marriage is redefined to include two men in love, on what possible principled grounds can it be denied to three men in love?[6]

He poses a valid question. We can take it another step. What could eventually prevent a person from marrying, say, an animal? Or an inanimate object?

This is the logical progression for a society that no longer understands what truth is. A generation ago, this was not only unthinkable, it was "un-thinked" (if I can invent such a word!).

Don't misunderstand; I'm not advocating a return to a "Golden Age," whatever that might have been. But I do know that at one time, society knew what truth was. Some might not have liked it, but they knew what it was. Now, however, we live under an entirely different set of circumstances.

Our job as Christians is to point the way back to truth. And to do it with love.

JOINING TRUTH AND LOVE

While the Gay Agenda strives to divide the family, to alter and destroy it, at the heart of our ministry must flourish both love and truth. Therefore, I will not stand at the door of our church and bar a gay man from entering. I also will not let him grow comfortable with a watered-down message from God's Word.

I once heard it put very well: "I am not showing love to a homosexual if I stand by while he practices his chosen lifestyle. In fact, the person who affirms and enables a person in the gay lifestyle in reality hates him. Why? Because while it is easier to let him continue in his sin, such a road leads only to destruction. It is much better to confront in love."

The son who returns home on a holiday and reveals to his father that he has a gay lover drives a wedge between himself and his parents. The clergyman who sermonizes that Paul affirmed homosexuality (the opposite of what he really taught) takes that church in his hands and rips it apart. The gay lobbyists in Washington who plead for same-sex marriages tear in pieces the fabric of our country.

If we have a genuine desire to heal these divisions, then we should happily minister to gays and their allies in both truth and love.

That's why our church has a ministry called HOPE ("Heal Our Pain, El Shaddai"). It was created by a couple in our church to provide hope for those who have a family member in the homosexual or lesbian lifestyle — a devastating thing for the entire family.

This support group meets weekly to allow its members to encourage one another and pray for one another as they stagger their way through this difficult challenge. It meets in a private and non-threatening setting.

Our church also has provided venues of ministry for families struggling with homosexuality. We have attempted to assist those in the gay lifestyle as well as those who are affected by it.

Do you know why we're doing this? We are neither condoning the gay lifestyle, nor are we shunning those involved. We strive to walk in obedience to God's truth *and* act in His love.

We have helped, are helping, and will continue to help people involved in the gay and lesbian lifestyle, as well as their families. We will

With one hand we will hold up God's truth and with the other hand we will hold up God's love for all people.

love them. With one hand we will hold up God's truth and with the other hand we will hold up God's love for all people. Our ministry is dedicated to closing up wounds, dismantling walls of separation, and leading with love and truth.

God loves all people; this I do know. He offers His unconditional love to each one of us, regardless of our sinful choices, even the sin of homosexuality. Still, although God unconditionally loves us, *that does not give us the right to disobey His commands and live however we please.*

With one hand, therefore, we grasp the truth of God, while with the other we take hold of the love of God. When those two are synthesized, the result ought to reveal the heart of every Christian and every Church in America.

THE HEART OF CHRIST

I think the church in America is faced with the continual question, "WWJD?" — What Would Jesus Do? All of us must answer this critical question.

God's Word, the Bible, makes plain what Jesus would do. Jesus would hold in one hand His truth, and in the other hand, His love. This is the heart of Jesus Christ. And it should be our heart, as well.

Bob Stith, a Texas pastor, learned how to minister to gays as he saw up close the misery unique to those trapped in a homosexual lifestyle.

> I've discovered that in ministry to homosexuals, *being* is often more important than *doing*. I share biblical truths, but most say what helps the most is having someone who simply loves them and will be there for them when they struggle and when they fail.[7]

As we decide how to deal with this great cultural divide at the beginning of the 21st century, it is vital that we maintain a biblical perspective. Dare to speak the truth! Dare to love! They're meant to go together.

Chapter 2

STATE OF
THE UNION

The life of Alexander the Great has fascinated Oliver Stone ever since the Oscar-winning film director was a boy. After a five-year hiatus from movie making, Stone is preparing to film an epic about the Greek ruler. *Time* magazine recently asked him about the project, including rumors of Alexander's bisexuality.

> I treat it as part of the story, not the whole story. Society had different standards in the pre-Christian era. Relationships between men were quite acceptable until a certain age, when marriage occurred.[1]

Stone is telling us that Alexander's alleged sexual preferences (which can't be documented from history) are simply another lifestyle choice. He exemplifies a passive response to non-traditional lifestyles.

Contrast his view with that of James Dobson, founder of Focus on the Family, as expressed on *Larry King Live*:

> That [same-sex marriage] will destroy the family, which will destroy the nation and I think eventually have a major impact on western civilization.[2]

These two views clearly show the widening divide in this country regarding gay issues. Various shades of opinion obviously exist between those expressed by Stone and Dobson, but without question the Gay Agenda is causing a massive split across all lines. Some voices are militant; some are reasonable; some are working mightily to repair the breach. Clearly, the state of the union is at stake. It makes one wonder if these really are *United* States.

Because of the aggressive nature of the gay lobby, events are changing so quickly that it seems no one has a firm grasp of the entire picture. One day I read about efforts of religious groups to block pro-gay legislation, the next about a lawsuit by two prison inmates who want to be allowed to marry — same-sex couples behind bars. The whole thing can feel overwhelming. Perhaps it would be instructive to review some key Gay Agenda gains.

LEGAL GAINS

After John Geddes Lawrence and Tyron Garner were fined under the provisions of a Texas sodomy law for engaging in homosexual acts, the pair sued the state. After a series of legal battles, the case ended up in the U.S. Supreme Court as *Lawrence v. Texas.*

On June 26, 2003, a legal and moral earthquake shook the nation when the U.S. Supreme Court ruled in a 6-3 decision that Texas's law against private, consensual sex between adults of the same sex is unconstitutional. This is the case responsible for catapulting the gay issue into its current high profile. This is why you are hearing and seeing it everywhere. Some believe it to be as profound a case as *Roe v. Wade*, the landmark decision that legalized abortion in this nation a generation ago.

Justice Antonin Scalia wrote a sharp dissent to his colleagues' decision in *Lawrence v. Texas*. He accused the court of having "largely signed on to the so-called homosexual agenda."[3] Scalia forecasted that "same-sex marriage" would be the logical next step.

That "next step" already has occurred. On May 17, 2004, due to a court order, Massachusetts became the first state to authorize gay marriage. Thousands of gay couples inundated the state's courthouses to apply for a marriage license. While Massachusetts is currently the only state to authorize gay marriage, New Jersey is expected to rule on a similar case soon.

These legal gains for the Gay Agenda did not come all at once. In 1993, the Hawaii Supreme Court ruled that barring same-sex couples from marrying may violate Hawaii's constitutional ban on sex discrimination. An Alaskan trial court in 1998 ruled that choosing a marital partner is a "fundamental right" and could not be interfered with by the state "absent a compelling reason." And three years ago, the state of Vermont became the first state to enact a law allowing same-sex civil unions.

Court decisions like these echo those that occurred previously in Europe. The Netherlands and Belgium already extend marriage rights to gay couples. Germany, France, Sweden, and Denmark also have "civil union" laws. Canada has signed on as well. The

The Gay Agenda is winning some major battles legally.

Canadian government was embroiled ina real showdown on this issue, with emotions running hot on both sides. A member of Parliament stated, "I've never seen an issue like this."

The Gay Agenda is winning some major battles legally.

POLITICAL GAINS

The Gay Agenda pushes on across America in multiple venues. Politicians are becoming increasingly more emboldened. What was unthinkable a generation ago has now become mainstream.

Six months before the watershed 2000 presidential election, Senate candidate Hillary Rodham Clinton strolled through Washington Square Park in New York. The occasion (on a Sunday) was a Gay Pride parade. Several state officials surrounded Clinton and then-New York Mayor Rudy Giuliani. Jubilant after political gains in upstate New York and Vermont, gays staged the parade as a celebration of a 1969 demonstration at the Stonewall Inn, which many believe set the stage for the modern gay-rights movement.

President George W. Bush has been caught in a major challenge in this issue. Yet, he stated courageously on July 30, 2003:

> I believe in the sanctity of marriage. I believe marriage is between a man and a woman, and I think we need to codify that one way or the other.[4]

The White House is supporting an amendment to the Constitution limiting marriage to being between a woman and a man.

Personally, I do not see any way to keep marriage defined as a union between a man and woman, unless a major spiritual revival occurs or a constitutional amendment is adopted, limiting marriage to a union between a man and a woman.

This action alone will take a miracle, and at least at this point in time, I would support it. If politicians attempt to tag on to the legislation other matters, however — such as recognizing homosexuality as an alternative lifestyle — then I would have to reconsider my support.

Many Christians have felt caught off guard by the "sudden" sweep across the land of same-sex unions, "gay marriages," and the like. What they don't realize is that, politically, winds of change have been blowing for a long time. This change has come largely from the top down.

During the 2000 presidential race, when contenders lined up behind the Democratic front-runner, Vice President Al Gore, candidates openly courted the gay vote. Richard Gephardt, congressman from Missouri, seemed particularly adept at this, hosting a fundraiser for the powerful Gay and Lesbian Victory Fund in Los Angeles. And in fact, Gore himself often held meetings with gay leaders, in the White House, and even asked a California assemblywoman for books that would help educate him and "sensitize" him to homosexual matters.

The former gay and lesbian outreach director for the Democratic National Committee, Brian Bond, realized the significance of this support:

> . . . both [Gore and Gephardt] are trying to send
> a message that our community is a member of the
> American family.[5]

When he came into office in 1993, Bill Clinton gained a reputation as a president who welcomed gays and lesbians. In 1996, he gave an interview which wound up as the cover story for an issue of *The Advocate*, a leading gay and lesbian magazine.

While Bush has clearly stated his position on traditional marriage, the 2004 Democratic nominee, Senator John Kerry, has waffled. Kerry told an MTV audience that while he believes people are born gay, he also thinks that, "some people might choose. . . ." He currently resists endorsing full marriage rights for gay couples.

If the most powerful leaders in Washington are still sorting out their views on same-sex unions, we must realize that major battles already have been won by the gay lobby in the last decade.

EDUCATIONAL GAINS

The University of Michigan offers a course called, "How to Be Gay: Male Homosexuality and Initiation." Professor David M. Halperin says the course does not teach students to be gay, but does teach them there are right and wrong ways to be gay.

New York City has created the nation's first public high school for gays, bisexuals, and transgender students. It began the 2003–04 school year with 170 students, tripling its enrollment from the year before.

In the Cambridge Friends School in Cambridge, Massachusetts, the Gay Agenda is front and center. Children in this entire school, even as young as five or six, celebrate Gay and Lesbian Day. In a school-wide assembly, a man named Jeff (a teacher), stood and said, "I can tell the truth that I'm a gay man. That gives me much more energy to be a better teacher, to be a better co-worker, and to be a friend." The students applauded, as if he'd canceled classes for a month!

If something does not change, this gay influence will take over our schools.

On his nationwide radio program, James Dobson recently called for Christian parents in California to leave the public schools. Why? Because public schools in the state of California are teaching a gay agenda beginning in kindergarten, all the way through the 12th grade. Long ago, the Gay Agenda became aggressive in our schools. Its champions realize that appealing to young people can go a long way in gaining acceptance of the gay lifestyle.

In the mid-'90s, producers Helen Cohen and Debra Chasnoff created a video designed for viewing in elementary public school classrooms. The documentary, *It's Elementary: Talking About Gay Issues in School*, was funded by the San Francisco-based Columbia Foundation, as well as People for the American Way, the Gay & Lesbian Alliance Against Defamation, and the California Teacher Association's Gay and Lesbian Caucus.

Chasnoff (who used the occasion of the 1992 Oscars to declare her lesbianism) is open about her agenda: "What's clear in the film is that the younger the kids, the more open they were. . . . If we could start doing this kind of education in kindergarten, first grade, second grade, we'd have a better generation."[6]

What's interesting about Chasnoff's view is that she is no doubt a fierce advocate of "toleration" for all world views — except, of course, mine. My world view says that this type of education is harmful for the young people she is targeting. Proponents of the Gay Agenda either fail to see or don't want to see the irony of their "intolerant tolerance." And make no mistake, they don't intend to go away. The Gay Agenda will not "go gently into that good night," but rather seeks sweeping changes in American culture.

Our schools are vulnerable because The Gay Agenda is winning some major battles.

MEDIA GAINS

Do you know what is happening on television? A new program, *Queer Eye for the Straight Guy*, features five gay men who call themselves "The Fab Five" who do makeovers on straight guys.

Another show, *Buy Meets Boy*, features a gay bachelor choosing 1 man from among 15 others, to be his partner.

The popular sit-com *Will and Grace* features several gay characters, and follows in the tradition of Ellen DeGeneres.

The infamous kiss between Britney Spears and Madonna during the MTV awards continues this erosion of traditional norms in our society. The goal of the Gay Agenda is to "baptize" you into its lifestyle, where it becomes normal for you to hear and see it, making you accept (eventually) that it is a non-threatening norm in our society.

Decades ago in Hollywood, a few might have known that stars like Rock Hudson were gay; but today, not only does most of the culture realize it — most people don't even react.

Joan M. Garry, executive director of the Gay and Lesbian Alliance Against Defamation (GLAAD), is pleased with new television shows like ABC's *It's All Relative* (a gay couple inter-acting with a college-age daughter) and Fox Channel's *A Minute with Stan Hooper*, in which two men operate a diner and con-sider themselves married.

For the first time on a broadcast network, the real-life experience of thousands of gay and lesbian families will be mirrored on television. My partner of 22 years and I can finally look at our three children and tell them there is a family on television that looks like us.[7]

Garry insisted that although there are no transgender char-acters, and only one new lesbian character for the fall line-up, "there are still areas of development."

This effort to push the Gay Agenda is across-the-board, with producers, directors, and actors joining the cause. In 2001, for example, writer/producer Aaron Sorkin (NBC's *The West Wing*), Tipper Gore, and actors Margot Kidder and Judith Light appeared at a media awards show at George Washington Univer-sity. The evening celebrated the advancements made by gay activist groups.

> *This effort to push the Gay Agenda is across-the-board.*

Outside of Hollywood, the established news media sub-tly promotes gay rights advocates as "the good guys" while depicting conservatives as insensitive at best, and dangerous at worst.

Former Massachusetts congressman Barney Frank has for many years been a flamboyant, outspoken gay politician; he often receives positive media coverage. His detractors, such as Texas congressman Dick Armey, are not so lucky. Armey once referred to Frank as "Barney Fag" and the gaffe, genuine or not, received much play on the networks. Gay rights advocates often talk about the "timeworn prejudices" of religious conservatives in Congress, a further attempt to marginalize America's mainstream views on gay issues.

And what about the ballyhooed claim of an unbiased media? It's a myth, as Associated Press writer Robert Tanner demonstrated when he wrote about gay couples in Oregon lining up to get marriage licenses in the spring of 2004:

> One hundred couples or more lined up around Oregon's Multnomah County office building Thursday morning, hoping for official recognition *of their love*[8] [emphasis added].

Their love. How's that for unbiased? A professional journalist decides and writes that gay unions are a product of "love." His words give us a glimpse into the entrenched bias in our country, torn apart by wide gulfs in world views.

The Gay Agenda has made some huge gains in the media.

ECCLESIOLOGICAL GAINS

The Gay Agenda is now making major advances into the Church. According to *USA Today*, five of the major denominations in America openly ordain gay clergy and bless same-sex unions. These are the Evangelical Lutheran Church, Presbyterian Church USA, Episcopal Church, American Baptist Church, and the United Church of Christ.

A national survey in the fall of 2003 gave an interesting picture of the attitudes of American churchgoers toward gay marriage:

> A new national survey of 1,515 adults, conducted Oct. 15–19 by the Pew Research Center for The People & The Press and the Pew Forum on Religion and Public Life finds that homosexuality in general — not merely the contentious issue of gay marriage — is a major topic in churches and other houses of worship. In fact, clergy are nearly as likely to address homosexuality from the pulpit as they are to speak out about abortion or prayer in school, say people who attend church regularly.[9]

According to the survey results, 80 percent of evangelical Protestants oppose gay marriage, while 54 percent oppose the choice. Fifty-five percent of Catholics oppose gay marriage, somewhat surprising given the church's staunch opposition to the gay lifestyle.

While the survey showed that societies in foreign countries — especially Europe — support gay marriage by huge margins, Americans are divided on this issue:

> A bare majority of Americans (51 percent) believe homosexuality should be accepted, while 42 percent disagree. In this regard, American attitudes have less in common with Western Europe or Canada than with Latin America, where opinion is also largely divided.[10]

The mainline churches are in deep turmoil over the issue, due to aggressive challenges by gay clergy. In response to the election of the Rev. V. Gene Robinson as bishop of the Diocese of New Hampshire (even though he is an active homosexual), the Rev. Sandye Wilson of the Minnesota Diocese exclaimed to the *New York Times*, "It's a great day for the church."

This newly elected bishop, with his daughter, Ella, and his sexual partner of 13 years, Mark Andrew, stated, "God has once again brought an Easter out of Good Friday."

One of the battlefields currently raging is found in the United Methodist Church. There, the debate surrounding gay issues could more properly be called all-out war. At the 2004 General Conference (the church-wide body that meets every four years), proponents and opponents of same-sex marriage took to the floor. The match that lit this fuse was struck earlier, with the church trial of Rev. Karen Dammann.

Damman, who admitted to Bishop Elias Galvan (on Valentine's Day 2001, no less) that she was a practicing lesbian, was tried by a 13-member jury several weeks before General Conference. The denomination's Book of Discipline clearly says that homosexuality is incompatible with Christian teaching, but incredibly, the jury acquitted Dammann!

The trial, the first of its kind in the UMC since 1987, created a firestorm of frustration on the part of conservatives. In fact, Rev. Bill Hinson, president of the one-million member Confessing Movement (dedicated to taking the mainline churches back to orthodoxy), proposed a split:

> We can't bridge the gap separating us. Our people,
> who have been faithful and patient, should not have to
> endure our endless conflict.[11]

The day after General Conference concluded, however, even conservative voices were backing away from talk of schism. The UMC, the second-largest Protestant denomination in the United States, with 36,000 congregations, has been in turmoil over the issue for decades.

In 1997, Rev. Jimmy Creech of First United Methodist Church in Omaha, Nebraska, performed a lesbian wedding ceremony. Bishop Joel Martinez promptly suspended him. In his trial, Creech gained acquittal by the thinnest of margins. Eight of the 13 jurors voted that Creech had violated the order and discipline of the church; nine votes were needed to convict.

Creech later said, "I believe that we can use the momentum of the trial to effectively challenge the anti-gay position of the UM Church at the General Conference in 2000. The great wall of bigotry may not fall then, but its collapse is inevitable, and we must be resolute at every stage and at every opportunity."[12]

We must be resolute at every stage and at every opportunity. That sword cuts both ways. It is incumbent upon every person who passionately defends traditional marriage to stay the course. Our opponents are networked, well-financed, and determined. We can do no less.

In a small meeting with some of America's leading pastors back in the spring of 2002, I heard James and Shirley Dobson, founders of Focus on the Family, speak. In our Q and A session with them, the question was asked of Dr. Dobson, "What is the number one issue and concern you have for the American family?"

Without hesitation, Dobson responded, "The number one issue for the family today is the homosexual activist agenda."

Events around the globe point up the accuracy of Dobson's words. In early May 2004, the papal ambassador to Madrid, Spain, delivered a stunning speech in front of Spanish bishops. He claimed that the Vatican had made a mistake in not supporting same-sex couples. Monsignor Monteiro de Castro, in the shadow of the church's statement that same-sex marriages are "evil and deviant," declared, "The new political situation . . . in Spain sets new challenges in the spreading of the gospel and we must meet those challenges in an appropriate manner." His speech still has observers buzzing.

Such "gains" for the gay lobby within the Christian community have emboldened it to further divide the church.

THE TEAR GROWS WORSE

The Gay Agenda is a blatant and pervasive attempt to destroy marriage and redefine it for everyone.

> *The Gay Agenda is a blatant and pervasive attempt to destroy marriage and redefine it for everyone.*

All of the examples just cited — from blatantly pro-gay TV, to misguided opponents of the gay lifestyle — demonstrate the painful tear in American society.

Truly, the state of this union is in need of healing, repair, and a return to sanity. And we have no more time to lose.

Chapter 3

THE GAY AGENDA

When *San Francisco Chronicle* reporter Rachel Gordon and photographer Liz Mangelsdorf walked into a growing national story inside the city's "sometimes sleepy" City Hall, they might have had visions of journalism awards. After all, San Francisco's mayor, Gavin Newsom, had made international headlines when he began issuing marriage licenses for same-sex couples on February 12, 2004 — just before Valentine's Day. For days, the major networks ran nightly stories on the avalanche of licenses issued in the exotic California city. A journalist's dream.

Instead, Gordon and Mangelsdorf found themselves pulled from covering the story, a decision handed down by *Chronicle* editor Phil Bronstein. The reason for the reassignment? Gordon and Mangelsdorf got married.

That's right; as 4,000 other same-sex couples "tied the knot" and then emerged on the steps of City Hall to face a sea of cameras, the two *Chronicle* journalists couldn't help themselves and also took part in a civil ceremony.

Initially, the two decided against the ceremony, since they didn't want a conflict-of-interest problem to arise. After a meeting with their editors, they decided to "marry."

According to Reuters:

> *Chronicle* editors agreed that "*Chronicle* journalists directly and personally involved in a major news story — one in whose outcome they also have a personal stake — should not also cover that story," the memo said. "It is that notion alone — being personally involved in such a specific way in the story one is covering — that drove our decision."[1]

This story would be funny in many respects, if it weren't so indicative of the pervasive nature of the Gay Agenda in America. True, Gordon and Mangelsdorf were upfront with their editors — and their boss pulled them off the story to avoid a conflict — but one can wonder how many other journalists, entertainers, politicians, judges, and educators push their pro-gay bias on a daily basis, with no recognition of the fact and no accountability for their actions.

OPRAH JOINS THE FRAY

In 1997, comedienne and actress Ellen DeGeneres "came out" on her television sit-com. Her character, Ellen Morgan, had a session with her therapist. Who played the therapist? Oprah Winfrey!

"Ellen, good for you — you're gay," said Winfrey. This endorsement, despite its fictional setting, amounted to a stamp of approval from one of our culture's leading icons. Oprah Winfrey has become identified as a source of advice for women everywhere. She now uses her power-base (one of the largest media conglomerates of all time) to push a pro-gay agenda. After years in the spotlight, "Talk-show host Oprah Winfrey realizes many women wish they could have her life."[2] She has become a genuine authority figure.

Ellen producers were not shy about their deeper agenda: targeting America's teens:

> Executive producer Dava Savel said, "If this episode helps some child in the Midwest with their sexual identification, we've done our job."[3]

It was Savel who suggested Oprah Winfrey to play the therapist, since "she's so well liked by the American people; it was perfect to have someone like her who connects with middle America, where if Oprah said it was okay, then it was okay."

Much of the entertainment industry has a clear and publicized agenda to promote gay issues. And DeGeneres and Winfrey are by no means the only ones doing so.

SUNDAY MORNING BLUES

Stephen Bennett has a fascinating story. Like so many trapped in a destructive lifestyle, he wandered in a lonely wilderness for years before leaving the gay lifestyle. Today, Stephen and his lovely wife, Irene, have two children, and have been happily married for over a decade. Little wonder, then, that producers from the CBS show "Sunday Morning" (hosted by Charles Osgood) called with an interview request. After all, Stephen Bennett is not only a great story, but a relevant one as gay rights issues are on everyone's minds.

Stephen relates that the CBS crew set up and the Bennetts were then interviewed. Naturally, not all of the 45-minutes of taping would be used — that's the nature of producing and editing television fare — but Stephen and Irene couldn't have imagined the final, "less than 60 seconds" interview would leave out the fact that Stephen Bennett used to be gay and now isn't.

Instead, they were portrayed as just another religious couple opposed to same-sex marriage and the gay lifestyle. Not a word about the freedom and deliverance he has experienced.

Now, why would producers extensively interview a couple like Stephen and Irene Bennett — a testament to the power of marriage between one man and one woman — and purposely edit out the central feature of their story?

It isn't hard to understand when we realize that entertainment figures in Hollywood and New York, especially, live and work among some of the most visible proponents of the gay lifestyle. Writers, producers, and editors in the entertainment industry promote the Gay Agenda because that's where they live.

Meanwhile, the vast majority — the rest of us — are often unaware of the ways in which televised stories are manipulated.

IT'S SHOWTIME

When Showtime, the cable channel, premiered "Queer as Folk" in 2000, one could suspect that the content would be highly inappropriate as family viewing. The program, featuring gay men discussing and engaging in sex, was meant to be provocative. Producer Tony Jonas said, "We pushed this as far as we could go."

That brazenness not only offended and outraged important media monitors like Donald Wildmon of the American Family Association — it also produced disgust that mainstream media outlets actually endorsed "Queer as Folk."

Wildmon says, "The country's moral fiber is quickly unraveling, and as bad as it has gotten on television in the last 25 years, I never thought I'd see the day when a TV series that shows men having anal sex would be applauded by *Time* magazine and *TV Guide*."[4]

Indeed, *Time* called the show "funny and fresh," while *Newsweek* called it "wonderful."

I urge you to pay attention not only to the examples of moral degradation in our society, but also to those who are promoting it.

I urge you to pay attention not only to the examples of moral degradation in our society, but also to those who are promoting such blatant bias.

A NOT-SO-GLAD GLAAD

GLAAD (Gay & Lesbian Alliance Against Defamation) is committed to staying the course in its pursuit of gay demands.

GLAAD's website has suggestions for media outlets that cover gay issues. Emphasizing "its human impact," GLAAD has a clever strategy: portray gays as human interest stories, rather than radical, "fringe" figures. The website is home to photos and stories that reflect this human interest angle. And that's not all of the public relations strategy:

> And given that the most vocal opposition to same-sex couples obtaining equal marriage rights comes from religious right political groups, consider reaching out to religious leaders who support marriage for gays and lesbians and who can distinguish between the civil and religious dimensions of marriage.[5]

In advancing this sophisticated PR campaign, GLAAD realizes that portraying gays and lesbians in Gay Day parades, as well as in bars and clubs, tends to project an image it would rather not emphasize. Instead, the focus should be on depicting gays "going about their daily routines." In other words, "normal."

This group also highlights every gain made by the gay lobby. In the spring of 2004, as a tidal wave of news coverage of same-sex marriage engulfed the country, GLAAD noted that the *New York Times* had begun publishing same-sex union announcements in its Sunday Style section; this after meetings with GLAAD representatives. These announcements are now placed in the country's top 25 media markets. Another glacier-like gain for the Gay Agenda.

GLAAD also understands that language is critical. Think of it as a war in which one air force dominates another; when you control the airspace, you control the war. The same can be said for language and communication. Those who control the message control the agenda.

GLAAD has even gone to the trouble of creating alternative definitions and terms. Labeling *gay marriage* and *traditional marriage* as "problematic," the "preferred" terms now have become *marriage rights for same-sex couples* or *marriage equality*. It all sounds so rational and fair.

Another disliked term, according to GLAAD, is *sexual preference*. The group prefers the subtle-but-vital change *sexual orientation*. A change of only one word, but in reality a paradigm shift. No longer is the gay lifestyle a choice; it is now beyond one's control. Just as one does not choose one's eye color, so too is one "gay by orientation." We must be aware of these efforts to re-frame the argument!

The American Humanist Association is another group that has long advocated for gay causes. In 1980, the group released its Statement on the Family, which called for "inclusion" and pushed for acceptance of gay and lesbian couples as constituting a family. Seventeen years later, the AHA reaffirmed its commitment: "The American Humanist Association reaffirms the validity and supports the legalization of same-sex marriages in all states of the United States."[6]

BOY SCOUTS GET PUMMELED

Sometimes, one feels that the struggle over the Gay Agenda is a fight to the death. One side will win, one side will lose. The conflict has extended even to that almost-sacred institution in America, the Boy Scouts. In 2000, James Dale, an assistant scoutmaster with a New Jersey troop, was removed from that position by the Boy Scouts, who said that Dale's gay lifestyle conflicted with the values promoted by the organization. Dale sued, and the case reached the U.S. Supreme Court. He lost.

I applaud the Supreme Court's decision in *Boy Scouts of America v. Dale*. It ruled, by a 5-4 vote, that a group can ban gay members if homosexuality is against its "expressive nature."

If the court had ruled otherwise, then churches and other private, religious-based organizations would have been legally pressured to hire gays, even if association with them would not have expressed our message. One vote kept that from happening in our country.

That same year, during a national political convention, a group of Eagle Scouts walked onto the stage and got booed and hissed. Why? Because the Boy Scouts have the right to ban gay leaders, due to the Supreme Court ruling.

But even though the Boy Scouts "won" the court case, they really lost. Since then, many in the corporate world have pulled their support. Government agencies pulled support. Community groups are constantly pressured to pull funds away from the Scouts.

These incidents teach us that the Gay Agenda is pushing hard against opponents, on many fronts. The message? *Stay away from the Boy Scouts of America and others like it that oppose the Gay Agenda.*

HITTING MAINSTREAM STATUS

One of the fascinating aspects of the cultural war over the Gay Agenda is that so many of its advocates have achieved "mainstream" status.

Time magazine recently recognized Evan Wolfson, executive director of the advocacy group Freedom to Marry, on its list of the world's 100 most influential people. Taking his place on a list that includes actor Mel Gibson, golf great Tiger Woods, and Tibetan monk the Dalai Lama, Wolfson surmised correctly that his place on the list "indicates more about advances in the gay movement's struggles for recognition than about him personally."[7]

As an attorney, Wolfson works to reach consensus about same-sex unions between gay and non-gay groups. His inclusion on *Time*'s list moves society a small step closer to inclusion for gays. On his website, Wolfson promotes the truth according to . . . Evan Wolfson.

> **Truth 1** — Ending marriage discrimination is, first and foremost, about couples in love who have made a personal commitment to each other, who are doing the hard work of marriage in their lives, caring for one another and their kids, if any. (Think couples like Del Martin and Phyllis Lyon who've been together more than 50 years.) Now these people, having in truth made a personal commitment to each other, want and deserve a legal commitment. Once the discussion has a human story, face, and voice, fair-minded people are ready to see through a second frame:

> **Truth 2**— The exclusion of same-sex couples from marriage is discrimination; it is wrong, it is unfair,

to deny these couples and families marriage and its important tangible and intangible protections and responsibilities. America has had to make changes before to end discrimination and unfair treatment, and government should not be denying any American equality under the law.[8]

THE FIGHT OVER ADOPTION

The ACLU (American Civil Liberties Union) is working overtime to promote gays and lesbians for adoption and foster care. Noting that "the last decade has seen a sharp rise in the number of lesbians and gay men forming their own families through adoption, foster care, artificial insemination, and other means," it follows that the very idea is, or at least should be, mainstream: "Researchers estimate that the total number of children nationwide living with at least one gay parent ranges from 6 to 14 million."[9]

The new poster girl for gay and lesbian adoption is Rosie O'Donnell, who has announced she is gay and already has adopted three children. She has become the new "role model" for gay parents and gay families and often is paraded as the new role model for the gay lifestyle.

In a 2002 interview, O'Donnell discussed her continual struggle with depression. And I can't help but wonder: could there be a correlation between her depression and her lifestyle?

POLLS SHOW THE TRENDS

A poll conducted for the PBS television show *Religion & Ethics NewsWeekly* shows that nearly half of America's evangelicals oppose a constitutional ban on gay marriage. This data is being used as a wedge by the gay lobby, which is using such information to promote the perspective that even America's religious culture is "mainstream" on the issue.

Anna Greenberg, vice president of Greenberg Quinlan Rosner Research Inc., the firm that conducted the poll, made an interesting comment about the poll results, which show that 52 percent "would prefer to rely on state laws to prevent gays from marrying rather than altering the U.S. Constitution." Her comment expresses an almost casual observance of the direction in which the cultural winds are blowing: "Evangelicals are just not that different than the rest of America."[10]

Notice that those polled do not *support* gay marriage; they just don't want to see the Constitution amended. Yet even these poll results are an attempt to marginalize the very real opposition to the Gay Agenda. The gay lobby is very good at using anything it can to divide the real mainstream, which is where the majority of Americans live.

The gay lobby is very good at using anything it can to divide the real mainstream, which is where the majority of Americans live.

A *New York Times* poll at the end of 2003 showed that 55 percent of Americans support a constitutional marriage amendment. And in early 2004, an ABC News/*Washington Post* poll on same-sex marriage indicated that "most oppose same-sex marriage, but balk at amending the Constitution." Fifty-five percent opposed same-sex marriage, but only 38 percent wanted to see an amendment to the Constitution.

A question asking if civil unions should be allowed showed a more even divide, with 51 percent agreeing to civil unions, with 46 percent opposed. *USA Today* reported in July 2003, that polls showing support for legal relations between gay couples had risen as high as 60 percent; only 35 percent of Americans did not support them.

After the *Lawrence v. Texas* Supreme Court decision, however, the polling numbers reversed themselves. People are now seeing the reality of the Gay Agenda's drive to take over the culture. It seems to take time for the American public to wake up on these issues.

Another survey by the Kaiser Family Foundation illustrates how the country is divided politically over same-sex marriage. Among those who "strongly oppose" same-sex marriage, 53 percent indicate they will vote for George W. Bush. Twenty-five percent favor the Democratic candidate, and a whopping 30 percent are unsure!

RE-IMAGINING THE BIBLE

Although we'll discuss the relevant biblical issues in chapter 6, it would help for the purposes of our discussion of the Gay Agenda to realize that the gay lobby is intent on re-imagining the Bible itself, with regard to homosexuality.

While discussing the Bible's prohibition of same-sex relationships, as outlined in Leviticus 20:13, for example, Paul Varnell notes that the passage does not address lesbian sex![11] As if lesbianism were therefore somehow acceptable. This "argument from silence," that if a particular subject is not addressed it subsequently is not prohibited, is faulty in the extreme.

Varnell then proceeds to tells us that Leviticus 18:22, which labels homosexuality as an "abomination," really ought to be understood by defining *abomination* as "a violation of cultic purity." And since in the Christian era we no longer operate under the rules of the Old Testament, the passage is irrelevant for today.

It gets worse — but you'll have to wait for chapter 6 to see how.

THE AGENDA ROLLS ON

We've seen that the Gay Agenda is rolling across the land, aggressive and effectively claiming victory after victory. The drive for the gay lifestyle to be accepted as normal and mainstream has scored decisive victories through entertainment, against venerated groups like the Boy Scouts of America, and through the determined efforts of organizations like GLAAD and the ACLU. One concerned commentator has carefully observed the Gay Agenda in action and has declared:

> For more than 40 years, the homosexual activist movement has sought to implement a master plan that has had as its centerpiece the utter destruction of the family. The institution of marriage, along with an often weakened and impotent church, is all that stands in the way of its achievement of every coveted aspiration. Those goals include universal acceptance of the gay lifestyle, discrediting of Scriptures that condemn homosexuality, muzzling of the clergy and Christian media, granting of special privileges and rights in the law, overturning laws prohibiting pedophilia, indoctrinating children and future generations through public education, and securing all the legal benefits of marriage for any two or more people who claim to have homosexual tendencies. These objectives that seemed unthinkable just a few years ago have largely been achieved or are now within reach."[12]

Seductive, sophisticated, and resolute, the Gay Agenda is also masterfully promoting division in our court system, as we'll see in the next chapter.

Chapter 4

THE COURTS AND ACTIVIST JUDGES

W hen Regina Rederford, an employee for the city of Oakland, California, posted a flyer at her place of work on January 3, 2003, little did she know that she would become embroiled in a lawsuit that serves as a microcosm of the country's culture wars. In fact, that's exactly where she finds herself, along with co-worker Robin Christy.

The flyer in question, titled *Preserve Our Workplace with Integrity*, promoted traditional values, including traditional notions of marriage:

> Good News Employee Associations is a forum for people of faith to express their views on the contemporary issues of the day. With respect for the Natural Family, Marriage, and Family values.

If you would like to be a part of preserving integrity in the workplace call Regina Rederford @xxx-xxxx or Robin Christy @xxx-xxxx."[1]

Even though the board where the pair had posted the flyer regularly saw a variety of views on social issues, supervisors immediately took down their flyer. It seems the women advertised a world view unacceptable to their superiors. A U.S. district court ruled that the two city workers could proceed with a suit against two supervisors.

This incident underscores the tremendous division in this country surrounding the issue of same-sex marriage. A seemingly routine posting on an employee bulletin board erupted into litigation, a case of employers having world views different from their employees.

A FEDERAL MARRIAGE AMENDMENT?

When Christians (and other conservatives) looked up and realized that a tidal wave of pro-gay initiatives was casting its long shadow over the country, many people scrambled to support a Federal Marriage Amendment. The strategy, supported by the president, would require amending the Constitution to define the institution of marriage as being between one man and one woman.

Because this issue is fluid and very far from settled, events were changing rapidly even as this book went to press. Opponents of the

Gay Agenda feel alarmed that the proposed amendment has been hanging in the balance, primarily for one reason: Congressional leaders face a huge public relations blitz from the gay lobby. Although some senators and congressmen will stay the course no matter what, many others will waver, depending

Congressional leaders face a huge public relations blitz from the gay lobby.

which way the political winds blow. They are not about to risk their careers in Washington. As Gary Bauer put it:

> My friends, we are at a crisis moment on Capitol Hill on the marriage issue. Many members of Congress report they are hearing more from the pro-homosexual marriage crowd than they are hearing from those of us who believe marriage should remain between a man and a woman.[2]

George W. Bush's speech on February 24, 2004, served to draw a line in the sand between the two camps. The president's courageous stand came down to this:

> After more than two centuries of American jurisprudence and millennia of human experience, a few judges and local authorities are presuming to change the most fundamental institution of civilization. Their actions have created confusion on an issue that requires

clarity. Our nation must enact a constitutional amendment to protect marriage in America.[3]

Opponents of gay marriage realized where the battle raged and acted quickly. Gay lobbyists counted on these proposals to die in committee, so that this greatest of issues for modern America would be left to the decisions of *unelected* judges around the land. These judges, like the rest of us, are biased humans. Do we really want major decisions like this to be made by these people?

Much is at stake and one can suppose that only the first shots have been fired in this latest culture battle. I expect that smoke on the battlefield will obscure the outcome for a long while.

LOOKING BACK AT THE GROUNDWORK

As I waded through research for this book, it became clear that the issue is creating deep fissures from coast to coast. Headlines such as "State AGs Come Down Against Gay Marriages" and "Judge Refuses to Stop Portland Gay Marriages" illustrate that almost unbridgeable gaps exist within the judiciary.

How did we get here? A glance at past court challenges in favor of gay marriage reveals that the groundwork for the Gay Agenda was laid decades ago:

- 1986: New York City's Human Rights Law is amended to prohibit discrimination against gays and lesbians, paving the way for equal rights for jobs, housing, and education.

- 1989: In *Braschi v. Stahl Associates*, New York's Supreme Court rules that so long as proof of a "committed relationship" can be established, same-sex partners qualify as "family" under the state's rent regulations.

- 1993: Hawaii's highest court rules that prohibiting same-sex couples from marrying "may violate Hawaii Constitution's ban on sex discrimination and can only be upheld if prohibition is justified by a compelling reason."

- 1996: A Hawaii trial court rules that "prohibiting same-sex couples from marrying is not justified by any reason, much less a compelling one, and that these couples should therefore be allowed to marry." Two years later, before the state's Supreme Court could issue a final ruling, voters amended the state constitution to allow the legislature to define marriage as being between a man and a woman, only.

- 1998: An Alaska trial court rules that it is a fundamental right to choose one's marital partner. Two years later, Alaska voters follow the Hawaii lead and choose to amend the state's constitution to restrict marriage to unions between men and women, only.

- 1999: Same-sex marriage issues in the courts shift to the east coast, where the Vermont Supreme Court rules that same-sex partners are entitled to all rights provided to married couples, under the state's constitution. The decision does not address same-sex marriage specifically, but is confined to rights and benefits.

- 2000: The Vermont legislature creates a law allowing "civil unions" for same-sex couples.

- 2002: Gay and lesbian couples in Massachusetts appeal a trial court's dismissal of a marriage lawsuit sought by said couples.

- 2002: Seven New Jersey couples sue in state court, asking for the right to marry.

While same-sex marriage issues seemed to emerge suddenly in 2003–2004, the groundwork had been laid years before. And today, court challenges, rulings, and controversial statements are exploding in courts all over the country.

THE LANDMARK DECISION

When the U.S. Supreme Court struck down a Texas sodomy law in 2003, the gay rights issue emerged front-and-center. The court's 6-3 decision reflected the shifting culture, because it reversed a 1986 ruling that states could "punish homosexuals for what such laws historically called deviant sex."[4]

The ruling was a key victory for the gay lobby, since it "enshrines for the first time a broad constitutional right to sexual privacy."[5]

Judge Anthony Kennedy spoke for the majority on the court: "The petitioners are entitled to respect for their private lives. The state cannot demean their existence or control their destiny by making their private sexual conduct a crime."[6]

A report by the Associated Press further reflected the nation's cultural changes. It said that while in 1960 each state in the union had an anti-sodomy law, today, lawmakers or courts have blocked or repealed the laws in 37 states.

In a reflection of the desire by many politicians (and/or appointed officials) to have it both ways, Justice Sandra Day O'Connor agreed with the court's decision, but did not vote to reverse the 1986 decision (in *Bowers v. Hardwick*). Justices Antonin Scalia, Clarence Thomas, and Chief Justice William Rehnquist dissented.

It is interesting to note that several of the justices who voted for the majority were appointed by Republican presidents, including Ronald Reagan and George H.W. Bush. That alone should make it clear that we cannot rely exclusively on people who *appear* to be of like mind with the majority of Americans, who do not support same-sex marriage. A similar issue is that of abortion; since 1973, conservative Christians have hoped in vain for a strategy to place judges and politicians who will steer the country toward a more conservative stance on social issues. It doesn't work!

In the decision for *Lawrence v. Texas*, Anthony Kennedy wrote:

> To say that the issue in *Bowers* was simply the right to engage in certain sexual conduct demeans the claim the individual put forward, just as it would demean a married couple were it said that marriage is just about the right to have sexual intercourse.[7]

He further declared that shifting opinion guides this court, and not the Constitution:

> The Texas statute undeniably seeks to further the belief of its citizens that certain forms of sexual behavior are "immoral and unacceptable." *Bowers, supra*, at 196 — the same interest furthered by criminal laws against fornication, bigamy, adultery, adult incest, bestiality, and obscenity. *Bowers* held that this *was* a legitimate state interest. The Court today reaches the opposite conclusion.[8]

Kennedy's italicizing of the word "was" speaks volumes. He means that the 1986 decision is no longer valid. Morals, even laws, change, according to Kennedy.

I will now quote at length the dissenting opinion, authored by Scalia, who clearly understands what's going on:

> Today's opinion is the product of a Court, which is the product of a law-profession culture, that has largely signed on to the so-called homosexual agenda, by which I mean the agenda promoted by some homosexual activists directed at eliminating the moral opprobrium that has traditionally attached to homosexual conduct.
>
> One of the most revealing statements in today's opinion is the Court's grim warning that the criminalization of homosexual conduct is "an invitation to subject homosexual persons to discrimination both in the public and in the private spheres." It is clear from this that the Court has taken sides in the culture war, departing from its role of assuring, as neutral observer, that the democratic rules of engagement are observed. Many Americans do not want persons who openly engage in homosexual conduct as partners in their business, as scoutmasters for their children, as teachers in their children's schools, or as boarders in their home. They view this as protecting themselves

and their families from a lifestyle that they believe to be immoral and destructive. The Court views it as "discrimination" which it is the function of our judgments to deter.[9]

Scalia prefers civil debate, not judicial dirty tricks (my phrase), and I concur. We do not want to persecute gays in this country, but, as Scalia said in his dissent: "Persuading one's fellow citizens is one thing, and imposing one's views in absence of democratic majority will is something else."[10]

Christian America wakes up from frequent naps and is astonished when it can no longer recognize the country.

This should be a wake-up call to opponents of the Gay Agenda. It seems that Christian America wakes up from frequent naps and is astonished when it can no longer recognize the country. The gay lobby has won some major battles and is, I believe, currently ahead in the war.

FALLOUT FROM THE RULING

In a *Washington Times* article that dealt with fallout from the Supreme Court ruling, conservatives who oppose the gay lobby were not deterred.

Lawrence [v. Texas] has set the stage, but the real action will begin when we see that decisive move made, probably this summer and probably in Massachusetts.[11]

That quote is from Matt Daniels, executive director of the Alliance for Marriage. Daniels believes that such judicial earthquakes are necessary to wake up sleepy Americans.

As debate about a constitutional amendment swirled around the country, Christians and other conservatives realized they were behind the curve with regard to agendas, tactics, and views concerning gay marriage. As the *Los Angeles Times* put it, opponents of gay marriage were "surprised and outraged" by an Oregon county's decision to issue marriage licenses to gays and lesbians.

The *Times* reported that "since 1992, voters have defeated three attempts to restrict gay rights. The votes were close, each time reflecting the cultural divide between liberal urbanites and conservatives living in the state's small towns and rural areas. Multnomah County, which encompasses most of Portland, is the most liberal and populous region of the state."[12]

Days after the story appeared, Multnomah County presiding judge Dale Koch ruled that a challenge to the issuance of marriage licenses to gay and lesbian couples, filed by the Oregon Defense of Marriage Coalition, was denied. More than a thousand licenses were issued that week.

The Oregon controversy provided a close-in view of the nationwide debate, with various opinions and conclusions being expressed. Coos County clerk Terri Turi would not issue licenses to gay and lesbian couples because it was "contrary to state law," while the ACLU's Dave Fidanque opined that couples who received a license in Multnomah County could be married "anywhere in Oregon."

Multnomah County Chairwoman Diane Linn admitted that she gave the order to issue licenses to gays and lesbians. Meanwhile, Commissioner Lonnie Roberts, who opposes gay marriages, said that he was left out of the discussions. He called it a "clandestine decision." Lynn has since apologized.

While the furor raged in Oregon, lawsuits sprang up like weeds in California, and Wisconsin and Kansas saw gay marriage bans "advance."

And so the divisions continued to multiply.

SERVANTS OF THE COURT

Like all of us, judges and elected officials are biased human beings. Their own views often color decisions. Usually they are reluctant to admit this, but New York Attorney General Eliot Spitzer is not.

"I personally would like to see the law changed," Spitzer said, "but must respect the law as it now stands."[13] His comment came on the heels of a flurry of attempts by same-sex couples to be married in several states in the spring of 2004.

California Attorney General Bill Lockyer came to many of the same conclusions that Spitzer did, even asking the state Supreme Court to "invalidate" same-sex marriages that took place in San Francisco. He acknowledged that he holds views similar to those of Spitzer:

What I hope will be helpful is to indicate that there is an equal protection claim that's at least partially valid. And that same-sex couples should enjoy all the rights and responsibilities of heterosexual couples. However, I think there is a legitimate legal basis for calling that civil union or domestic partner. In our state, it's an argument about the word marriage.[14]

Their comments should be enough to recognize that state officials' opinions do not differ appreciably from the justices who sit on the U.S. Supreme Court. They are not interpreting law, but rather expressing their own feelings. And what have we done about it?

So far, not much.

INACTION BY CHRISTIANS

James Dobson understands that, so far, Christians have not effectively engaged themselves in this battle against the Gay Agenda.

> This apocalyptic and pessimistic view of the institution of the family and its future will sound alarmist to many, but I think it will prove accurate unless — unless — God's people awaken and begin an even greater vigil of prayer for our nation.
>
> As of this time, however, large segments of the Church appear to be unaware of the danger; its leaders

are surprisingly silent about our peril (although we are tremendously thankful for the efforts of those who have spoken out on this issue). The lawless abandon occurring recently in California, New Mexico, New York, Oregon, Washington, and elsewhere should have shocked us out of our lethargy. So far, I'm alarmed to say, the concern and outrage of the American people have not translated into action.[15]

This despite polling done by George Barna, which reveals that by a two-to-one margin, Americans reject the idea that the Bible does not specifically condemn homosexuality.

To some degree, we know what we believe — but inaction on the part of "average" Christians is harming our defense against the Gay Agenda. And that inaction, in great part, has brought us to where we are today, scrambling to overcome the smooth-running, networked, aggressive gay lobby.

Chapter 5

POLITICAL CHAOS

E tta White knows a thing or two about civil rights. And the plain-spoken African-American didn't take kindly to John Kerry's intimation that he does, as well.

At a campaign stop in the Mississippi town of Tougaloo, White, 74, took the Democratic presidential nominee to task for comparing the drive for gay rights with the folks who faced down the water hoses and attack dogs of Bull Conner.

> Most of the people in this country are sick and tired of the onslaught of the homosexual community using the civil rights movement to further their own agenda.[1]

Kerry, in a town hall meeting, sought to link the beating death of Matthew Shepard with the equally horrific murder of

James Byrd, Jr., an African-American who was murdered in Texas when three white men offered him a ride home, then beat him, slit his throat, and dragged his body behind a pickup truck. The grisly killing, on June 7, 1998, prompted agonizing flashbacks for many civil rights activists, who remembered only too well the violence of the 1950s and '60s.

Kerry, perhaps uncomfortable away from the sea spray of Cape Cod, somehow felt the need to appear empathetic to an audience that had lived the civil rights movement. The Massachusetts senator took his turn:

> Let me tell you something: when Matthew Shepard gets crucified on a fence in Wyoming only because he was gay, when Mr. King gets dragged behind a truck down in Texas by chains and his body is mutilated only because he's gay — I think that's a matter of rights in the United States.[2]

That Kerry misidentified Byrd as "King" is a harmless slip of the tongue from a weary candidate invoking a legendary civil rights leader, but it's nowhere near as interesting as his Clinton-esque portrayal of Byrd as "gay." That's news to everyone. Byrd was savagely killed in a crime of prejudice, but Kerry's tortured linkage of Byrd with the gay movement was a clumsy attempt to engage his audience.

Not yet finished with the senator, Etta White made perhaps the greatest observation that anyone has yet drawn in this divisive culture war:

> My point is, homosexuality is an idea. You have never heard a doctor say, "Mr. And Mrs. John Doe, you have a bouncing baby homosexual." It's an idea.[3]

My point is, homosexuality is an idea. You have never heard a doctor say, "Mr. And Mrs. John Doe, you have a bouncing baby homosexual." It's an idea.

Homosexuality as idea. How profound. The failure to see it as such reflects the current political chaos and cultural confusion in this nation.

ZIGZAGGING ON THE ISSUE

Candidates from both great American parties often zigzag on the issue of gay rights. At least one can respect the unambiguous attitude of Ralph Nader, who, when asked his view on same-sex marriage, responded gruffly that he "isn't much interested in gonadal politics."[4] Nader, one can assume, doesn't stand a chance of becoming president (although he's been a candidate more than once), and perhaps his honesty is a key reason.

With the gay issue white-hot in American politics, we shouldn't spend too much time assessing the views of the current front-running candidates for president. What is important to remember is that political leaders from the very beginning have had gay staff members, have circulated gay issues, and no doubt have held definite opinions on the issue. Also, who can say that the stances of the current presidential challengers are more important than those of future aspirants to the office? This issue might be with us in 20 years, and you can bet that politicians will be all over the map then, too.

Our polarized culture, however, has pushed George Bush and John Kerry into a glaring spotlight. It has stuck to other presidential hopefuls like tar, as well. Former Democratic challenger John Edwards, senator from North Carolina, voiced his opposition to both gay marriage and same-sex unions, proving that the issue is not strictly across partisan lines. As we have seen, the president has made his stance clear, going so far as to advocate a constitutional amendment to define marriage as being between one man and one woman.

Kerry has taken a more traditional (at least in terms of the last few decades) view, telling a fundraising audience in San Francisco that he supports the idea of the federal government recognizing same-sex unions if they are legalized on the state level.[5] If this became reality, such "couples" would be eligible for the thousands of benefits available now to married couples.

The senator, who galloped away from his competition during the spring Democratic primaries, has straddled the fence on the gay issue. Often he has said that while he personally opposes same-sex "marriage," he espouses views such as those in San Francisco. He stands in opposition to the president on the proposed federal marriage amendment, and "was one of only 14 senators in 1996 to vote against the Defense of Marriage Act"[6] (ironically, signed into law by one of our nation's most "gay friendly" administrations, under President Clinton).

The division over the Gay Agenda, of course, goes far beyond presidential politics. It has spread far and wide to both the state and local levels.

New York Governor George Pataki is a prime example of the weaving and dodging so prevalent among many politicians. But why should this surprise anyone? He has a wide constituency and voters are all over the political map themselves. Consequently, politicians such as Pataki stake out a view on gay rights that in reality becomes views, plural.

According to the *New York Times*, "Gay activists see Governor George E. Pataki as one of the best governors in the country on issues that matter to them, even though he insists that marriage should be between a man and a woman only. That position puts the moderate Republican governor in the same camp as many conservative Republicans — and moderate Democrats — across the nation."[7]

FAULT LINES EVERYWHERE

The cultural fault lines are evident everywhere, and politics is no exception. In the fall of 2003, the Wisconsin legislature, controlled by Republicans, passed a constitutional amendment banning same-sex marriage. Democratic Governor Jim Doyle vetoed it!

Soon after, the similarly "Republican-controlled Indiana senate passed a state marriage amendment, but watched the Democratic speaker of the house declare it dead on arrival."[8]

The *Baptist Press News* has noted the following:

- President Bush supports a federal marriage amendment; Democratic presidential candidate, John Kerry, opposes it.

- DNC Chairman Terry McAuliffe has said an amendment would introduce "discrimination" into the Constitution. Republican National Committee Chairman Ed Gillespie has said his party "must pursue whatever policy is necessary" to protect the definition of marriage.

- The large majority of amendment co-sponsors in Congress are Republicans. Of the 100-plus House co-sponsors, more than 90 percent are Republicans.

- Senate Majority Leader Bill Frist (R-Tenn.) supports an amendment. Senate Minority Leader Tom Daschle (D-S.D.) opposes it.

- The Democratic state parties of Massachusetts and New York have gone on record as officially supporting same-sex "marriage."[9]

Could we find a better picture of the serious split in our country over this issue?

A LACK OF POLITICAL WILL

Craig Mitchell, a professor of Christian ethics at Southwestern Seminary, believes that politicians will not necessarily decide the gay marriage issue based on the views of their constituents. He says that "politicians and the media were unwilling to side with the majority of Americans who believe in the God-given and traditional definition of marriage."[10] He also noted that 66 percent of Americans "fundamentally oppose same-sex marriage and that the media, except FOX News, had done all it could to bring the situation about."

FOX News also pointed out that "social policy has always been divisive in the Republican Party, which relies on the backing of both social and fiscal conservatives. Abortion, gay marriage, and other social issues have been hard to sell to more moderate Republicans."

An intriguing insight into this hesitancy of will on the part of many Republicans was discussed on *The O'Reilly Factor*[11], when host Bill O'Reilly questioned Byron York, White House correspondent for *National Review*.

O'Reilly had earlier made the point that President Bush seems reluctant to take on social issues (acknowledging that he has what might be perceived as larger issues to deal with, such as the war on terror). York responded, "Well, you know, fighting the culture war is simply not George Bush's thing. He's not inclined to do it. If you remember back to the 2000 campaign, his platform was basically, I want to cut your taxes and bring everybody together."

O'Reilly asked why York held this opinion, and the correspondent gave two answers: a) the president realizes they are very divisive issues, and b): "The other thing is, personally I believe Bush comes from a religious background in which it's a very contemporary, Christian non-judgmental kind of faith. You know, it's kind of in the Democrats' interest to try to portray him as a fire and brimstone member of the religious right, but that's simply not him. And I think he doesn't like these divisive fights."

Perhaps what York has stated is true, but it also may be his own interpretation of some matters. We need to remember, the president is the president of the entire nation. Therefore, he cannot be blatant about every issue. Yet, the unique and commanding thing about President Bush is that he is against abortion, against cloning, and is risking his presidency on supporting a constitutional amendment about marriage being that of only a man and woman. Without question, this is highly commendable in this bending leadership culture in American politics.

UNAFRAID TO SPEAK OUT

In the spring of 2004, Senate Majority Leader Bill Frist said that Congress must act "and act soon" to prevent local officials from "redefining marriage for everyone." He added that proponents of traditional marriage didn't seek or "relish" the fight over the advancement of the Gay Agenda. He referred to the issue as a "wildfire."

Nebraska Attorney General Jon Bruning, addressing the Senate judiciary subcommittee on the Constitution, warned that actions taken in Massachusetts and elsewhere threatened to force states to comply with the issuance of same-sex marriage licenses. Ironically, and pointedly, over 70 percent of Nebraskans voted four years earlier to amend the state constitution to define marriage as being between one man and one woman, yet the aggressive gay lobby, in the form of the American Civil Liberties Union and the Lambda Legal Foundation, challenged it in federal court.

While the wildfire raged on Capitol Hill between leaders like Frist and those who were signaling their lack of political will on same-sex issues, a few politicians around the country stood up to the Gay Agenda. In Massachusetts, of all places, Governor Mitt Romney's spokesman, Eric Fehrnstrom, said in response to the decision to marry out-of-state gay couples, "What next, is

Provincetown going to start marrying ten year olds in violation of the law?"[12]

The *Boston Globe* reported that while the governor opposes the same-sex unions in his state, "Romney faces increasing resistance statewide from city and town clerks, who are refusing to follow the governor's demands that they deny marriage licenses to out-of-state same-sex couples after gay unions become legal next week."[13]

Truly, the political landscape at this point in American history genuinely reflects chaos when it comes to the issue of same-sex unions. It is up to committed citizens to put out this "wildfire" through prayer, political vigilance, and efforts to repair the terrible division in our nation.

WHERE ARE THE EVANGELICALS?

Bob Reccord, president of the North American Mission Board, reported in May 2004, that he and other pro-family leaders met with lawmakers to discuss the proposed Federal Marriage Amendment legislation. He noted that while the gay issue is raging across the country, congressional leaders expressed puzzlement at the lack of involvement by one side of the voting public.

Speaker of the House Dennis Hastert has recently stated that Capitol Hill is hearing very little response from the grassroots and, therefore, assumes that it must not be a very big issue among the general populace.

We must change this impression!

Right now our concerns about how the gay rights movement may restrict religious freedoms here are being played out in Canada. Our friends to the north already have embraced gay marriage and the Canadian Parliament has recently passed a law adding homosexuals to the list of those protected from so-called "hate speech."

Reccord touches on two key issues. First, the lack of communication from conservatives frustrates him. Why the silence?

We have to keep in mind that a pro-family father or mother is preoccupied with the daily routine: working, taking care of children, church activities. They are at a disadvantage, since proponents of gay marriage, generally speaking, have no such responsibilities. Whereas a pro-family dad works in a factory or as an accountant or as a high school football coach, many pro-gay men work for the ACLU or as professional lobbyists on Capitol Hill or act on a popular television series. In other words, many pro-gay individuals are "married" to their cause and have ample time to lobby, write, and speak out. This is a disadvantage that must be overcome through sheer diligence. We must make time to contact our congressional leaders and make our voices heard.

Second, the threat to our free speech liberties is very real. Canada provides a disturbing model for what we can expect. The

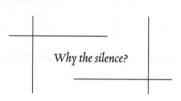

Why the silence?

POLITICAL CHAOS

day might soon come when a pastor, speaking from the pulpit, will be in danger of committing a "hate crime" if he upholds the scriptural teaching about homosexuality. Or imagine the discrimination lawsuits if our local churches are faced with hiring a person who turns out to be gay! Should our church be obligated to hire, say, a practicing homosexual?

I know that many of our fellow Christians are occupied with the business of raising their families and staying involved in church, school, and neighborhood activities. They may be trusting that this issue will take care of itself. But with some congressional leaders wavering on these votes, every voice is greatly needed.

Make sure yours is heard.

ADDRESSING THE BIBLICAL ISSUES

Chapter 6

T ony Campolo is one of the most entertaining speakers in the Christian community. If you haven't had an opportunity to hear Tony in person, you've missed out, as they say.

In his book *20 Hot Potatoes Christians Are Afraid to Touch*, Campolo tells a poignant story involving a minister asked to preach the funeral of a gay man who had died of AIDS.

It seems that this pastor from an inner-city church felt somewhat at a loss as to what to say. When he walked into the funeral home, he saw a few dozen gay men. They appeared to be frozen — not speaking, hands in laps, staring straight ahead. Their grief gave the room a heavy feeling.

On the ride to the cemetery near Hoboken, New Jersey, the pastor continued to feel overwhelmed by this sad occasion. At the conclusion of his graveside remarks, he turned to walk away, but one of the deceased man's friends stopped him. Would the pastor read the 23rd Psalm? He did so, and then found himself deluged with requests for other verses of Scripture.

Reading from the eighth chapter of Romans, in which Paul tells us that nothing can separate us from the love of God, the pastor noticed that the color had returned to the men's faces. They clung to the truth that nothing can separate us from the love of our Creator.

I relate this story because it tells us several things.

On one level, it is simply a story of hurting humanity, something we all know about.

On another level, it gives us an important insight into the gay community — the part of the gay community that, as Campolo says, is hungry for the Word of God, but would not set foot in a Bible-believing evangelical church. Why not? The answer is obvious:

"They feel that Christians despise them."[1]

I would probably disagree with many things that Tony Campolo believes. He has a reputation for being "too soft" on issues important to conservative evangelicals. Many Christians either denounce this talented professor of sociology or, at best, feel uncomfortable with the theology that allows him to reach out to the gay community to an unusual degree. But at least on two things relevant to the gay culture, I can agree with him:

- Much of Christendom despises homosexuals;
- We ought not behave that way.

Does my stance confuse you? I suspect that it may bewilder folks like Tony Campolo, as well. I appear to want it both ways: to welcome people who choose to live a gay lifestyle, while upholding Scripture.

You know what? I believe we *can* have it both ways. In fact, I believe we *must* have it both ways. Allow me to articulate what I believe is a balanced, biblical position. But first, let's note where we have arrived at this stage of history.

HAS GOD MADE IT CLEAN?

In an article in the *Northwest Arkansas Times* titled "All God's People," subtitled "Local Episcopal Church Officials React Positively to Appointment of Church's First Gay Bishop," one of the pastors of St. Paul's Episcopal Church said:

> "What God has made clean you must not call profane." Grisham quoted from Acts 10. He said that blessing same-sex relationships of two people who plan a life-long dedication should not be considered less.[2]

Claiming Acts 10 as a justification for same-sex marriage and for the ordination of gay bishops is one of the worst distortions of Holy Scripture I have ever heard in my life. Acts 10 tells us that God wants to reach out in love to men and women of all races across the globe, not that He has re-evaluated and corrected His position on a sin He formerly labeled "an abomination."

The good news is that not all Episcopal churches follow such a flawed and unbiblical line of reasoning. Many press reports suggest that meetings already have taken place among many national Episcopal leaders who want either to change what has happened in their denomination, or sever their connection to it. We need to pray for these men and churches to remain strong in their very turbulent environment.

Despite stories like this, and even though the Gay Agenda has won some major battles legally, politically, educationally, and ecclesiologically, there *is* good news. And part of it is that the Gay Agenda will never win biblically and theologically.

WHAT DOES THE BIBLE SAY?

Champions of the Gay Agenda can and do try to twist the Scriptures to their advantage, or at least to cause enough doubt in regard to issues of interpretation that they can effectively cloud what God has to say on the issue. But they will never finally accomplish either goal. God's Word will always accomplish the purpose for which *He* sends it:

> As the rain and the snow
> come down from heaven,
> and do not return to it
> without watering the earth

and making it bud and flourish,

so that it yields seed for the

sower and bread for the eater,

so is my word that goes out

from my mouth:

It will not return to me empty,

but will accomplish what I desire

and achieve the purpose for which

I sent it (Isa. 55:10–11).

And what does God's Word say about the practice of homosexuality? To begin with, in both Leviticus 18:22 and 20:13, God calls homosexuality an abomination. And what is an abomination? An abomination is an outrage, a disgrace, something detestable to God — and this is what God says the practice of homosexuality *is*.

In Romans 1:26–28, the Bible twice says of practicing gays and lesbians that God "gave them over" to their sin, meaning that he let their sin run its destructive course in their lives. Their rejection of God's truth results in enslavement to ungodly passions, which eventually and inevitably leads to a terrible judgment at the hands of a Holy God.

An abomination is an outrage, a disgrace, something detestable to God — and this is what God says the practice of homosexuality is.

Such debauchery occurs when women are engaged sexually with women and men are engaged sexually with men. God gives such a person over to a debased mind, which means He allows him or her to sink to the depths of their degenerate lifestyle. In other words, God lets their sin run its course, which always results in ruin.

In 1 Corinthians 6:9–10, we learn further that those who practice the homosexual lifestyle will not inherit the kingdom of God. Paul expressly tells those who actively practice such a lifestyle, "Do not be deceived. Neither the sexually immoral nor idolaters nor adulterers nor male prostitutes nor homosexual offenders . . . will inherit the kingdom of God." And why would the Apostle tell his readers, "Do not be deceived"? Answer: Because many people *are* so deceived. They think they can practice these things and still reach heaven. Paul says they can't.

We should bear in mind that this passage also names a few other sins in the same context; the emphasis throughout is on practicing those sins, meaning they have become one's habit, one's lifestyle; this is what one has become.

The Word of God declares homosexuality to be a sin and indicates that all those who practice it need to be saved from its grip by the strong arm of Jesus Christ. And our Lord has the power to make that rescue happen! For in verse 11, Paul declares that some of his readers once had to be saved from exactly this sinful lifestyle. "And such were some of you," he writes. Listen to this same passage from other versions of Scripture:

> A number of you know from experience what I'm talking about, for not so long ago you were on that list (The Message).

> There was a time when some of you were just like that (New English Translation).

> Some of you used to be like that (Contemporary English Bible).

In Greek, the word translated "such" is the term *tauta*. This is a nominative, neuter, plural form of the demonstrative pronoun. A simple translation of it is "these." Because it is a neuter form, the word "things" can be supplied in English; thus, it can read "these things." This is significant, because Paul is not referring to these Corinthians as people, but as things. It is as if their sin had grown so deeply entrenched in their lives that they were known specifically for it. They practiced it; it was their lifestyle; that's how they thought of themselves. And Paul says that if these things are practiced as a lifestyle and no repentance takes place, genuine salvation in Jesus Christ has not occurred.

This text should remind us that we are not against gays and lesbians, but against the terrible sin that blinds them. Paul tells his friends, in essence, "Some of you were living that debauched lifestyle, but now you are washed by the blood of Jesus. Now you have new life. You are sanctified by the Holy Spirit and are being transformed into brand new individuals. You were justified, set free from your sin and now wear the robes of Jesus' righteousness. Therefore, you must no longer dress in the garments of your sinfulness. To the glory of Jesus, the Holy Spirit has done and is continuing to do a great work of transformation in all your lives."

Paul further reminded his readers that because God had washed, sanctified, and justified them, they couldn't go back to the sins from which they had been saved. How could they live for the very things that had caused Jesus to die on the cross? How could they celebrate what God hated? In verses 9 and 10, Paul lifts up the banner of God's truth. In verse 11, he raises the banner of God's grace.

While I could comment on a number of other biblical passages that clearly condemn homosexual practice, I believe the ones just noted are sufficient for our purposes here. For those who would like a more in-depth look at the issue, I recommend several books: *A Strong Delusion*, by Joe Dallas, and *Straight & Narrow: Compassion & Clarity in the Homosexuality Debate*, by Thomas Schmidt (both

> *The bottom line is this: The Bible nowhere affirms, sanctions, endorses or approves the practice of homosexuality.*

IVP); and "Responding to Pro-Gay Theology" in the *OneByOne Pastoral Care Guide*, available from Exodus International.

The bottom line is this: the Bible nowhere affirms, sanctions, endorses or approves of the practice of homosexuality. God never calls it an alternate lifestyle. God opposes civil unions of homosexuals. God condemns same-sex marriage. God is against the ordination of homosexuals into the ministry. *Never* does God authorize any practice or act of the gay lifestyle.

That means that same-sex marriage is an abomination to God and any such "matrimony" is unholy, ungodly, and will receive the judgment of God. Same-sex marriage is nothing more than an attempt to redefine one of the holiest ordinances of God, marriage between male and female.

Do not forget that Jesus himself said, "at the beginning the Creator 'made them male and female,' and said, '*For this reason a man will leave his father and mother and be united to his wife, and the two will become one flesh*'" (Matt. 19:4–5, italics added). For what reason did God create marriage? Only one is given here: God made human beings male and female. Therefore, only a man and a woman can become "one flesh" in marriage.

NOT EVERYONE AGREES

I indicated in chapter 3 that a major effort is underway by proponents of the Gay Agenda to discredit biblical injunctions against the practice of homosexuality, or at the very least to throw enough dust in the air to make the Bible's testimony on the issue seem unclear. The work of Paul Varnell serves as an example of this effort.

An article by Varnell claims, "Levitical condemnation of male homosexuality has been hugely influential. But its meaning is ambiguous, and it may have applied to a supposed practice — Canaanite religious prostitution — that never occurred at all."[3]

Ambiguous. Remember that word, because it is used in this context as a battle axe to divide the church on the issue of homosexuality — and not just in regard to Old Testament passages, but equally to ones in the New Testament.

One Methodist scholar has said in this regard, "As for me, I have ambivalence — which was once regarded as the supreme Methodist theological virtue! I just don't know. I cannot disregard Paul's anthropology, but I do not understand why he speaks against same-sex relationships."[4]

John Shelby Spong thinks he does know why Paul spoke against same-sex relationships. His outrageous comments seem designed to do nothing but fling dirt into the air in order to confuse naïve readers:

> Since Paul framed the primary Christian concept
> of grace, would it not be a life-giving insight to suggest
> that all of us received that sense of grace, understood
> as the unbounded love of God who loves us just as we
> are, from one who had been a repressed and self-hating
> homosexual man?[5]

While Spong's suggestion is blasphemous in the extreme (and without a shred of evidence), I'm sorry to say that his views can no longer be considered "fringe." One has only to visit a seminary, a secular university, or even a local church to make this sad discovery.

In fact, Spong and other radical "scholars" like him regularly get invited to churches near the University of Arkansas campus, only minutes from our church. And they are succeeding to a large degree in spreading confusion about the Bible's clear teaching.

Bob Stith, the Texas pastor I quoted in chapter 1, recognizes the corrosive effect the gay lobby has had on many people in this country:

> I've seen mothers and fathers, family members and friends, even sincere pastors who have drifted into some level of acceptance of homosexuality because they have not been presented with a genuine redemptive model. Some unwittingly accept the belief that homosexuality must be genetic, and God would not call it sin if He made them that way.[6]

Of course, God did not "make them that way," but opponents of the church's traditional teaching on homosexuality want you to think He did. And they often use a couple of common strategies to make their case.

Critics of the traditional view of the Bible's opposition to homosexual behavior often insist that the Old Testament's prohibitions against homosexual practice applied only to ancient cultures (if, indeed, they applied even to them). They claim that opposition to homosexuality on the grounds of these texts is so outdated as to be laughable.

To take it further, they claim that citing these passages puts Bible advocates in a difficult position. Their question usually sounds something like this: "Okay, so you say the Bible calls homosexuality an 'abomination' before God. Fine. But will you 'literalists' also insist on upholding all the Mosaic law, even stoning disobedient children?"

Remember the scene from a popular television program that I quoted early in the book? The fictional U.S. president used this very argument not only to humiliate a political opponent, but to cleverly use it as a wedge issue among Christians. I've seen many Christians stopped in their tracks by this argument. Let's examine it briefly.

IT PROVES TOO MUCH

First, such an argument "proves" too much. If we are to toss out biblical injunctions against a particular behavior simply because those prohibitions are found in the (supposedly outdated) Old Testament, then should we not also throw out its commands against murder, theft, and rape? After all, those commands are also found in the (supposedly outdated) Old Testament.

So far, I don't know of anyone (yet) who wants to do that. But do you see what this means? In that case, it means that everyone agrees that at least *some* of the Old Testament's prohibitions are still valid and in full force. The primary question is, which ones are and which ones aren't?

I would argue that the best place to start making such a determination is in the New Testament. And what do we find there? We find at least three texts (Rom. 1:26–28; 1 Cor. 6:9–10; 1 Tim. 1:9–10) that explicitly condemn homosexual practice. And we also find that *nowhere* does the New Testament approve of, sanction, or look positively at a gay lifestyle.

Second, I would point out that everywhere we look in the New Testament, we find the same testimony: the *only* kind of intimate sexual activity that God endorses occurs between a husband (male) and his wife (female). So the writer of Hebrews writes:

> Marriage should be honored by all, and the marriage bed kept pure, for God will judge the adulterer and all the sexually immoral" (Heb. 13:4).

In New Testament times, when this passage was written, the word "marriage" meant *only* a wedded union between a man and a woman. Therefore, the only kind of sexually active "bed activity" that God smiles upon occurs in the marriage bed, that is, between a husband and his wife. When it comes to sex, no other kind of bed can be considered "pure." *Nothing* else qualifies.

Third, I might point out that although the New Testament confirms and continues the Old Testament's condemnation of homosexuality, it does not stipulate or authorize any kind of corporal punishment for this sin; it leaves that in the hands of God. While both Jesus and Paul instructed believers to separate themselves from professing brothers or sisters in Christ who engage in a blatantly sinful lifestyle (see Matt. 18:15–17 and 1 Cor. 5:1–13), such church action is intended to be remedial, to bring the sinning individual back into a right relationship with God and with the fellowship of believers (see 2 Cor. 2:5–11).

Fourth and finally, I might refer to a scholarly tome by Robert A.J. Gagnon titled *The Bible and Homosexual Practice*, which does a thorough job of showing why and how these ancient texts cannot so easily be thrown out of the argument. Gagnon does us all a great service by demonstrating not only the proper historical context of these passages, but also their continuing relevance.

A LONG TIME IN COMING

It is worth noting that the Gay Agenda has been with us for a very long time. It has been developing in the shadows, waiting for the just right moment to step into the daylight.

In a *Time* magazine piece back on July 26, 1963, the canon of England's Southwark Cathedral was quoted from a sermon he delivered:

Christ nowhere suggested that marriage was the only place where sexual relationships could take place . . . a great deal of prejudice against homosexuality is on the grounds that it is unnatural. But for whom? Certainly not for the homosexual.

This man's words make it clear that many years ago — long before Bible-believing Christians realized what was happening — proponents of the Gay Agenda already were introducing a set of morals different from the norm. Those morals have brought us to where we are, scrambling to dislodge entrenched efforts to accept homosexuality as an "alternate lifestyle."

Many years ago . . . proponents of the Gay Agenda already were introducing a set of morals different from the norm.

Proponents of same-sex marriage and the ordination of actively gay clergy use every methodology possible to promote this sinful lifestyle. Appealing to one's humanity, to one's emotions, and to one's sense of compassion is what I would call "a tactic."

Witness an "open letter" from the Rev. William Sloane Coffin to former NFL great and current minister Reggie White. You may recall that White took quite a beating from the press in 1998 after he addressed the Wisconsin state legislature, telling its members, "We've allowed this sin [homosexuality] to run rampant in our nation, and because it has run rampant in our nation, our nation is in the condition it's in today."

In his letter, Coffin took White to task for his comments:

> I write you all this in large part because today the "gay agenda" has replaced the "communist threat" as the battering ram of reactionary politics. It grieves me to see you put your considerable muscle behind such a blunt instrument of prejudice.[7]

Where did Coffin get his unbiblical views on homosexuality? Perhaps his uncle, Henry Sloane Coffin, the one-time president of Union Theological Seminary, nudged him in that direction. The elder Coffin had a hand in the commentary sections of *The Interpreter's Bible*, a set of volumes on biblical theology that for decades has served (primarily) the mainline churches.

In *The Interpreter's Bible*, for anyone with time to wade through the weighty (I'm using a literalism here!) books, one can find the most radical revisionist scholarship. Bible characters such as Jonah and Job, for example, are routinely considered mythical. Eventually, this abhorrent theology made its way to the nation's pulpits.

And what is the significance of all this for us? Namely this: once the authority of Scripture is weakened, the great moral questions of any era become clouded, as well. And that is where we are today. The same men who performed their radical theological surgery on Scripture 80 years ago were the spiritual ancestors of men like Spong, Marcus Borg, John Dominic Crossan, and others who today sow spiritual confusion, even about God's views of homosexuality.

Consider the views of Virginia Ramey Mollenkott, professor emeritus of English at William Paterson University. Over the years she proposed a number of interesting theories to an unknown number of impressionable students. In her own words:

> Not only did Jesus pointedly praise all of those who for various reasons did not marry and bear children, not only was the baptism of one such person pointedly described in Acts 8:26–40, but Jesus performed a miracle on behalf of a Roman Centurion who was distraught over the illness of a boy who may have been his lover (Matt. 8:5–13).[8]

One struggles to respond adequately to this type of wild and baseless teaching. Yet this school of thought has traction in our culture. To impressionable college freshmen, it seems authoritative and quite possible. It is also quite false.

I can say that my beloved Arkansas Razorbacks have won dozens of national football championships, but it isn't true. It isn't supported by the facts, so my bias and passionate agenda to promote my bias are built on nothing but lies and wishful thinking.

In fact, there is *no* evidence that Paul or the Roman centurion were gay. Yet the Gay Agenda has found both contentions to be useful as propaganda tools within the church. We must be aware of this kind of despicable scholastic trickery and refute it both skillfully and lovingly.

REASON FOR THANKS

Thankfully, there are scholars and religious figures who not only know the truth, but who courageously promote it.

Dennis Prager makes an interesting point about the current push for same-sex marriage in the United States, highlighting a fact that the gay lobby would prefer to ignore: "There was not one major religious leader or thinker in Jewish or Christian history prior to the present generation who argued for same-sex marriage."[9] One might well ask, "Why not, if the biblical passages on the issue are so 'ambiguous' "?

Russell D. Moore, dean of the school of theology at the Southern Baptist Theological Seminary in Louisville, Kentucky, has written an important article in which he makes several good points in regard to gay rights and the Bible.[10] Moore understands that it is not our business to argue the authority of Scripture with our gay rights opponents, but simply to stand on the truth of Scripture while holding up true morality and the basis for it:

> Our pulpits communicate well the "wrongness"
> of same-sex unions. But too often we sound like a

"constituency" arguing for our rights to the status quo. We speak about what is at stake for "our" marriages and "our" families — and all that is true. But we should speak more about what is at stake for those tempted to follow the lie of homosexual liberation. The apostle Paul reveals to us the outcome: death (Rom. 1:32). That truth should make our hands tremble and our eyes moisten.

Moore ably articulates our dual obligation: speak the truth, and speak it in love. We love homosexuals and our fervent prayer is for them to come to know their Creator, as He reveals himself in His Word. Hear Dr. Moore again:

> We should oppose same-sex "marriage" not just because we believe Romans 1, but also because we believe John 3:16. And the culture should see us as brokenhearted revivalists, not just outraged moralists. We shouldn't see homosexuality simply as a threat to family values in the abstract. We should weep that it is also a Roman road to hell — for real people with faces [and] names.[11]

God calls His church to love gays and lesbians through their struggles. The homosexual community will certainly love them into error; we need to love them into truth. Here's how we should respond to the Gay Agenda:

- Hold up God's truth without shame or compromise.

- Declare the gospel message of liberty and hope.

  God calls His church to love gays and lesbians through their struggles.

- Help even our children and student ministries to demonstrate love and help to those struggling with their sexuality.

- Demonstrate God's mercy and love to those in the lifestyle of homosexuality and to their families, without a hint of compromise.

While I warmly invite those who practice homosexuality to attend our church — in the hope that God will convict them of their sin and prompt them to draw on God's grace for salvation and the transformation it brings — yet no practicing homosexual can serve in a ministry or lead in any capacity in our church.

THE WORST OF SINNERS

The good news is for each one of us, regardless of our past, our sins, or our present. It tells us that we can be washed by the blood of Christ and given a new life in Jesus. We can wear the robes of His righteousness. And we can be freed, acquitted from all our sins.

All sin is wrong. But only one sin determines whether you go to heaven or hell when you die — the sin of rejecting Jesus Christ as your Savior and refusing to allow Him to live actively and daily as the Lord of your life.

Jesus Christ died on the cross to forgive our sins and to set us free from the penalty of those sins. He became sin for us. He became sin for *you*.

Friends, *this* is the chief message of the Bible. *This* is the good news. And *this* is what the apostle Paul lived and died for:

> Here is a trustworthy saying that deserves full acceptance: Christ Jesus came into the world to save sinners — of whom I am the worst. But for that very reason I was shown mercy so that in me, the worst of sinners, Christ Jesus might display his unlimited patience as an example for those who would believe on him and receive eternal life (1 Tim. 1:15–16).

And that's a Bible passage that ought to get all of us shouting, "Amen!"

Chapter 7

CULTURES
IN DECLINE

J erusalem, A.D. 70. A Roman soldier stands on the burly shoulders of another and tosses a lit torch through a window of the temple. Almost immediately, a raging fire engulfs the magnificent structure. As the soldier admires his destructive handiwork, he cannot help but hear the shrieks and moans of terrified Jews, accompanied by the mocking laughter of his cohorts. And so the awful calamity prophesied by Jesus Christ unfolds, exactly as He predicted it almost 40 years before (Matt. 24).

We know something of this terrible event from the writings of Josephus, a first-century Jewish historian and an eyewitness to the carnage. Perhaps, as he watched the destruction of Jerusalem at the hands of the Tenth Roman legion, he also thought of past civilizations — not only their magnificence, but also their decay: Canaan, Egypt, Assyria, Babylonia, Greece.

A modern observer, Malcolm Muggeridge, has certainly thought of society's tendency to decay:

> I conclude that civilizations, like every other human creation, wax and wane. By the nature of the case there can never be a lasting civilization anymore than there can be a lasting spring or lasting happiness in an individual life or a lasting stability in a society. It's in the nature of man and of all that he constructs to perish, and it must ever be so. The world is full of the debris of past civilizations and others are known to have existed which have not left any debris behind them but have just disappeared.[1]

All great cultures fall into decline. Rome's own grisly end came in the fifth century, with the coming of the barbarians.

As these ancient cultures shuffled off into oblivion, most of them shared many similarities: rebellion against God, reliance on slavery; conquest and the injustices that followed; eventual boredom and a collapse of vigilance.

It is also true that these civilizations decayed from within. Specifically, these ancients (except the Jews) in their twilight years embraced homosexuality. Large numbers of Greeks and Romans, in particular, gave themselves over to this lifestyle.

You probably knew that. But does it surprise you to hear that, in early Greece, homosexuality was against the law? It really was. Yet change agents began to erode the values that Greek society possessed and, eventually, the end came. Rome later followed, and for a time at least, embodied the rule of law. By her end, though, the mighty empire wheezed and staggered and crashed. A soft life and habits of excess drove a stake through the Roman heart.

The fact is, *no culture in history* that has embraced homosexuality has long survived. The gay lifestyle is simply not the way to build a healthy society.

WHERE IS AMERICA?

Jim Nelson Black, in his book *When Nations Die*, identified ten factors that bring about a civilization's collapse. Read this list and tremble.

- Increase in lawlessness
- Loss of economic discipline
- Rising bureaucracy
- Decline in education
- Weakening of cultural foundations
- Loss of respect for traditions
- Increase in materialism
- Rise in immorality
- Decay of religious belief
- Devaluing of human life[2]

Black believes that only a handful of these characteristics are enough to bring a culture crashing down. And he maintains that, for the first time in history, a single culture — the United States — possesses all of them at once.

Where is America today? It is a chilling question, is it not? Is this still "Christian America"? Kerby Anderson, founder of Probe Ministries and a co-host of *Point of View*, sees the handwriting on the wall. "Apart from revival and reformation," he declares, "this nation is destined to decline."[3]

EXTREME IN EVERY WAY

There's no question that observing American culture is both frightening and fascinating.

The current youth generation tells us a lot about America. It does what every other generation in history has done, namely, it reflects the culture that gave it birth. And one word more than any other probably describes this generation: extreme. It is extreme in every way.

The youth of this nation are extreme in sports. No longer is it good enough simply to take a football and throw it around. No longer is it good enough to shoot a basketball through a hoop. This generation likes to jump out of airplanes. It likes to climb dangerous mountains. It likes to hang glide.

This generation is also extreme in knowledge. Its members grew up with the Internet and the WorldWide Web and know how to access all the secrets of the Information Age. These "tekkies" are extreme in technology. They understand that at very tip of their fingertips, sitting in front of the computer, they can access the entire world in a matter of moments.

And why is this generation so extreme? It is so because it reflects the culture in which it lives. Right now, all across this country, extreme events grab the headlines. As a nation we are seriously considering whether to approve of gay marriages. It's already begun in one state,

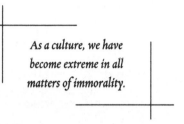

As a culture, we have become extreme in all matters of immorality.

Massachusetts, and it's threatening to flow across to the others. As a culture, we have become extreme in all matters of immorality.

Would any of us have seriously believed, a generation ago, that we would be facing the myriad issues surrounding gay marriage? It has come on us like a hurricane. I'm not sure how it came upon the ancient Greeks and Romans, but I am sure that the end result will be the same for us as it was for them.

WE'RE NOT ALONE

I don't mean this as a comforting thought, but we are not the only decadent culture in the world today. Unfortunately, we're not alone; we're not even necessarily leading the way. Western cultures across the globe are in decline.

I've read that in London, what once were great and vital cathedrals are now either museums or mosques. Doesn't that blow your mind?

In Paris, you'll see an anything-goes society. Not only homo-sexuality, but a sexually permissive society at all levels. In May 2004, the French prepared to go even further when a Socialist party leader declared his intention to amend French statutes so that same-sex couples would be granted equality with hetero-sexual couples.

Socialist leader Francois Hollande will ask his par-ty to draft new laws to recognize civil marriage for all applicants, regardless of gender. Such a law would ex-pand on the Civil Solidarity Pact (PACS), which was instituted in 1999 and confers on unmarried couples — same-sex and different-sex — many of the same benefits married couples receive.

PACS does not, however, provide full adop-tion rights and tax breaks to same-sex couples. "Ev-ery society should be organized on the principle of equal rights and respect," Hollande told the Agencie France-Presse. "Marriage should be open to every-body."[4]

France's Justice Minister, Dominque Perben, said that no such marriages would be legally recognized — but one suspects that, even though they are not recognized *now*, and that adop-tion rights and tax breaks are still an open question . . . it is only a matter of time.

Visit Stockholm and you'll see not only state-sanctioned gay marriages, but every manner of sexual depravity. That culture is on the brink of collapse and its citizens seem unaware. One of the claims made by proponents of gay marriage, such as Jonathan Rausche, an American, is that gay partners allowed by the state to marry will so appreciate the right that they will not easily give it up. He expects much lower divorce rates among homosexuals than among heterosexuals.

But early data from Sweden does not look good for his prediction. The Institute for Marriage and Public Policy conducted a study that showed legalized gay marriages in Sweden actually suffer dramatically *increased* numbers of divorces as compared to the heterosexual population. The study, "Same-Sex Unions and Divorce Risk: Data from Sweden," was an eye-opener:

> Same-sex legal unions, however, had unusually high rates of divorce. Sweden is a country with relatively low rates of marriage and relatively high rates of divorce. In 1999, 55 percent of Swedish births occurred outside of marriage. There were 53 divorces for every 100 marriages.

The study found that gay male couples were 1.5 times as likely (or 50 percent more likely) to divorce as married opposite-sex couples, while lesbian couples were 2.67 times as likely (167 percent more likely) to divorce as opposite-sex married couples over a similar period of time. Even after controlling for demographic characteristics associated with increased risk of divorce, male same-sex couples were 1.35 times as likely (35 percent more likely) to divorce, and lesbian couples were three times as likely (200 percent more likely) to divorce as opposite-sex married couples.

On another front, consider Europe's attitude toward children. In Portugal, an adult can get sexually involved with a child as young as 13. In the Netherlands, the legal age is 12!

Yet another sobering example of the decay of European culture occurred in December 1999, when the European Court of Human Rights "affirmed the rights of gay parents to care for their children."[5]

The case that sparked the debate occurred in 1994, when Joao Manuel Salgueiro de Silva Mouta was awarded parental responsibility by a Lisbon court. His ex-wife refused to let him see their nine-year-old daughter after she learned that de Silva Mouta was living with another man. The Lisbon court ruled that homosexuality was "an abnormality, and children must not grow up in the shadow of abnormal situations." It allowed de Silva Mouta visiting rights, but would not grant the same to his male partner. He was also barred from revealing his living arrangements to his daughter.

That decision was reversed five years later, with the Euro court ruling in Strasbourg, France.

The European court said that the ruling was a gross violation of Article 8 of the European Human Rights Convention and that it trampled upon "respect for private and family life" the court is sworn to uphold.[6]

It all reminds me of the grim passage in Isaiah — "Woe to those who call evil good and good evil, who put darkness for light and light for darkness, who put bitter for sweet and sweet for bitter" (Isa. 5:20). No longer is homosexual behavior unacceptable in the culture. Now it is the refusal to embrace the gay lifestyle that has become unacceptable!

All of Europe reeks of moral relativism. Truth can be my truth and it can be your truth, but the two don't have to be the same. For many decades now, Europe has watered down biblical truth; the divisions that exist over the Gay Agenda have simply existed there longer than they have here. But the same relativism and decay that stains Europe has now reached America.

NEEDED: A WAKE-UP CALL

Sticking our heads in the sand will not help. We cannot simply "wish" our culture a longer life. Union University President David S. Dockery has said:

> *Sticking our heads in the sand will not help. We cannot simply "wish" our culture a longer life.*

> People today may not want to hear this, but the contemporary vision of a "user friendly" God is not

the God of truth, the holy God who has made himself known in Christ. We must understand that these
are not just cultural controversies that we can ignore.
Much is at stake for the sake of the gospel, the church,
and our society.[7]

If we want to head off a cultural collapse, we need a serious
wake-up call. I like Kerby Anderson's attitude:

> Nations rise and nations fall. Every nation has fol-
> lowed this progression from bondage to bondage. The
> nations of this century will be no different. But let us
> not accept the Marxist notion that these are fixed and
> intractable laws of history. Christians can point to un-
> usual times when revival has redirected the inexorable
> decline of a civilization. In the Old Testament, Jonah
> saw revival postpone God's judgment of Nineveh. In
> the 16th century, Martin Luther and John Calvin saw
> a Protestant Reformation transform Europe. And even
> in the history of the United States the First and Sec-
> ond Great Awakenings changed individuals and our
> society.[8]

Sexual immorality has stalked and defiled every great culture, from the beginning of time to now. Pornography has existed in "primitive" forms for thousands of years; it was here
during Colonial days. Lust has shadowed men and women,

great and common. Early Hollywood was just as sexually corrupt as it is now — its stars just didn't have CNN camped on their doorstep.

Gradually, over many years, we have sunk to our current degree of sexual decadence. Now it is upon us, in full power. The winds of change are strong and the sands of corruption are aloft.

A thousand years from now, will a new superpower look back in wonder at the demise of the great United States of America? Or will this nation live on, indivisible, with liberty and justice for all?

I, for one, believe there may yet be hope.

A REASON FOR HOPE

Although he was open to gays in his administration, former President Bill Clinton signed into law the 1996 Defense of Marriage Act, which stated that "the federal government will not recognize a homosexual union sanctioned by a state and that no other state has to accept a homosexual 'marriage' performed in another state."[9]

Because few things in America are set in stone, this seemingly clear legislation sits on a foundation of sand.

> But both proponents and opponents said they expect courts to rule the law unconstitutional, because the Constitution requires states to give "full faith and

credit" to contracts, including marriage contracts, from other states. So the amendment's backers say that amending the Constitution is the answer.[10]

As we saw with the Supreme Court's reversal of its 1986 decision, time is the most important ally of the gay lobby. But since the 1996 law was enacted, opponents of same-sex marriage feel that congressional support is still there: at that time, the bill passed 85-14 in the Senate, 342-67 in the House of Representatives.

On another front, Pope John has said that gay marriages performed by clergy "degrade" what he calls the "authentic Christian family" (I like that term!). In February 2004, the Pope said:

> This is a time in which there is no lack of attempts to reduce marriage to a mere individual contract, with characteristics very different from those that belong to marriage and the family, and that end up degrading it as if it were a form of accessory association within the social body.[11]

It seems that more and more in these matters, it is the church body in Africa that stands on moral clarity. After the shameful installation of Rev. Gene Robinson as the first openly gay bishop in the Episcopal Church, the archbishop of the Anglican Church of Uganda sent a letter to Frank Griswold, the presiding bishop of the Episcopal Church in the United States. I quote at length a portion of that letter:

Considering those things, we were shocked to receive a letter from you informing us of your decision to send a delegation to the enthronement of our new Archbishop in January, and your intention for the delegation to bring aid and assistance for the people who live in desperate conditions in the camps in Gulu that you have ignored for years. Recent comments by your staff suggesting that your proposed visit demonstrates that normal relations with the Church of Uganda continue have made your message clear: If we fall silent about what you have done — promoting unbiblical sexual immorality — and we overturn or ignore the decision to declare a severing of relationship with ECUSA, poor displaced persons will receive aid. Here is our response: "The gospel of Jesus Christ is not for sale, even among the poorest of those who have no money. Eternal life, obedience to Jesus Christ, and conforming to his Word are more important. The Word of God is clear that you have chosen a course of separation that leads to spiritual destruction. Because we love you, we cannot let that go unanswered. If your hearts remain hardened to what the Bible clearly teaches, and your ears remain deaf to the cries of other Christians, genuine love demands that we do not pretend that everything is normal. As a result, any delegation you send cannot be welcomed, received, or seated. Neither can we share fellowship nor even receive desperately needed resources. If, however, you repent and return to the Lord, it would be an occasion of great joy.[12]

That letter leaves me almost speechless. Praise God for the Ugandan church, which is a light to us all!

I also thank God that there are real leaders in the renewal movements within the mainline denominations, such as Bill Hinson, the Rev. James Heidinger (Good News), Diane Knippers (of the Institute on Religion and Democracy), and Mark Tooley (UMAction). Tooley, in fact, performs a valuable service by monitoring the statements of gay activists all across the church and then informing the laity through various articles he writes.

It is also interesting to note that while the United Methodist Church is considered in many quarters to be one of the more liberal Protestant denominations in America, this seems to stem more from the institutional takeover by liberals than by theological abandonment on the part of the laity. There is real effort being made by the laity to bring the church back to its roots. We should keep these groups and individuals in our daily prayers.

We should also continue to pray for such voices of sanity as Chuck Colson, James Dobson, James Kennedy, and others, who give me hope that the Gay Agenda is not destined to be victorious in our culture. Kennedy, whose Presbyterian stance and evangelical message ring out from his headquarters in Ft.

Lauderdale, Florida, is a breath of fresh air. He, too, recognizes the importance of godly leadership in high places:

> I am deeply grateful for the president's long-awaited and unequivocal endorsement of a federal marriage amendment. His support will go far to ensure that Congress acts this session to pass and send to the states an amendment that will remove this matter from activist judges and renegade public officials. The wildfire of lawlessness that has erupted in San Francisco and New Mexico must be contained. The passage of a federal marriage amendment will ensure that no judge or elected official will take it upon himself to redefine marriage for the rest of America.[13]

Dobson has fought for family values for almost 30 years as head of Focus on the Family; he calls the struggle over the Gay Agenda "the climactic moment in the battle to preserve the family, and future generations hang in the balance." It doesn't matter that secularists and humanists "don't get" Dobson; he is a visionary who clearly understands the biblical and cultural issues surrounding the Gay Agenda.

And there are additional positive signs that, across the Christian culture, some people "get it":

- Beverly Heights United Presbyterian Church, in Pittsburgh, Pennsylvania, has voted to sever ties with ten regional governing bodies in eight states over repeated attempts by church leaders within the PCUSA to overturn a law that bans homosexual clergy. In 1997, the PCUSA added a proviso to church law requiring all clergy to either observe "fidelity in heterosexual marriage" or "chastity in singleness." Since then, many liberal church leaders have attempted to repeal the law.[14]

Praise God for Beverly Heights and those who take similar stands!

- Eleven years after his retirement from the church, a former bishop received a sanction from the Episcopal Diocese of California for marrying his same-sex partner, according to the Associated Press. Reverend Otis Charles, who served as Episcopal bishop of Utah for 15 years before retiring in 1993, received notice from Bishop William Swing that he would lose his license to perform church ceremonies as a result of his April union with his partner of two years.[15]

The Southern Baptist Convention and the United Methodist Church both unambiguously declared in 2004 that homosexual acts are contrary to Scripture, and reaffirmed their opposition to homosexuality, the ordination of sexually active gays, and consecrating same-sex unions.

Leaders, movements, and events like those just outlined give me hope that this battle can yet be won. And I take courage from more ancient stories that recount similar battles fought against long odds. I think of Nehemiah and the tremendous opposition he faced from powerful and well-entrenched enemies. His reverent words found an honored place in the Word of God:

> They were all trying to frighten us, thinking, "Their hands will get too weak for the work, and it will not be completed."
>
> But I prayed, "Now strengthen my hands" (Neh. 6:9).

There is work yet to do.

Now it is our turn to pray the same thing: "O Lord, now strengthen our hands." For there is work yet to do.

A FINAL WORD

> *If I profess with the loudest voice and clearest expression every portion of the truth of God except precisely that little point which the world and the devil are at that moment attacking, I am not confessing Christ, however boldly I may be professing Christ. Where the battle rages, there the loyalty of the soldier is proved, and to be steady on all the battlefield besides is mere flight and disgrace if he flinches at that point.*
>
> — Martin Luther

A cold wind blows the old man's white beard, whipping dry leaves past his weathered face. He shivers as his closed eyelids wrinkle, flicker, then open slowly. It has been a good, long nap for Rip van Winkle. As he rises to stretch, his joints feel unusually stiff. One hand touches the rough bark of the tree against which he's been reclining. With the other, he strokes and smoothes the beard he didn't have when he fell asleep.

As he squints in the direction of the town below, an odd, strange realization dawns on him: he's been asleep far longer than a few hours. And the world around him has changed! The frightening truth slaps him fully awake — and contributes to the numbing coldness he feels.

My friends, *our* name is Rip van Winkle. This beloved folk story is about *us*. The fact is, the Church was sleeping and aging at the birth of the Gay Agenda. And by this late hour, that agenda has gained energy, motivation, and a big head start. The Gay Agenda does not have truth, family, and the Church.

THE SPIRIT OF THE AGE

The German word *zeitgeist* is sometimes used to denote "the spirit of the age." If the speed at which the Gay Agenda is gaining momentum has stunned you, then you need to wake up to the fact that the spirit of the age, its *zeitgeist*, is against us. And those who believe that homosexuality is a sin, that the gay lifestyle falls far short of God's perfect intent for any person in this world, will be known as extremists.

We have to realize that the rules and definitions are changing unbelievably fast. Judges, courts, and various officials are forcing their world views on us all by their idiosyncratic interpretations of the law. The world is changing, and we had better wake up soon.

May I remind you that we are not talking about whether the White House should be painted another color. We are not talking about environmental issues. We are not discussing the latest alert from the Homeland Security Office. We are not debating an editorial In the *Wall Street Journal* or the *New York Times*.

We're talking about a fundamental issue that no one can afford to ignore.

While liberal courts and reformist judges may make their decisions based on the shifting moral sands and changing winds of our culture, we cannot alter our foundational belief in marriage and family just because some cry for "freedom" at all costs. We must remember what the Apostle tells us about these kind of activists: "They mouth empty, boastful words and, by appealing to the lustful desires of sinful human nature, they entice people who are just escaping from those who live in error. They promise them freedom, while they themselves are slaves of depravity — for a man is a slave to whatever has mastered him" (2 Pet. 2:18–19).

True freedom is not choosing what you want to do, but doing what you ought to do. We are most free when we remember that while God will forgive mistakes, He will not forgive rebellion.

Great division over this issue of same-sex marriage exists in our families, in our churches, and in our nation. In fact, the great divide is Grand Canyon-size and growing — and if we sit silently or treat this issue with indifference, a generation from now, the divide will make the Grand Canyon look like a tiny creek bed.

As large as this divide has grown, however, it is in our power to bridge it. We can do so by holding the Word of God in one hand and the love of God in the other.

As large as this divide has grown, however, it is in our power to bridge it. We can do so by holding the Word of God in one hand and the love of God in the other.

Scripture tells us that the Creator is both unchanging and unmovable. He does not take polls to see what He ought to consider righteous behavior for this week. That is why we don't have to wring our hands and wail that all is lost. *It is not.*

WHAT TO DO NOW?

So what should we do? Continue to sit under the thinning shade of a dying oak, stroking our beards and wondering, *what happened?* Or something else?

I believe that those of us — the vast majority — who believe that traditional marriage alone forms the backbone of human civilization must forget the wasted time of the past and *act now.* We have no more time to lose.

It is past time that we sound the alarm, blare the trumpet, and rally the troops who believe that marriage is between a man and a woman. If we allow marriage to be redefined to include same-sex couples, the Twin Pillars of Morality and Spirituality — which have served as beacons of the American culture since our beginning — cannot long stand.

While it may take us only a few short years to rebuild the shattered Twin Towers of New York City, this nation has spent more than 228 years building itself on that which is spiritual and moral. If we lose this battle over same-sex marriage, it may take generations to regain the true American heritage: a biblical commitment to marriage between a man and a woman. And we will have forfeited the wonderful privileges of being part of an America where the family can grow strong, healthy, and happy.

We do not have to let that happen. While the Gay Agenda has won some major battles in our land, the war continues to rage on. If we are to turn the tide, we have to act on several fronts:

• *Pray*

These times call for prayerful, peaceful engagement on this issue. Pray with passion, interceding for the soul of our nation like you have never prayed before!

• *Educate yourself*

No matter who you are and no matter where you are, you are capable of educating yourself about biblical issues. You are capable of processing information and applying Scripture to your life and to the lives of those with whom you come into contact. Pay attention to the pastor who preaches about this issue during his Sunday sermon. Read your newspaper. Watch the nightly news and try to get a balanced presentation from all the networks. If you have Internet access, log on to such sites as the American Family Association (<www.afa.net>); Focus on the Family (<www.family.org>); the Ethics and Religious Liberty Commission of the Southern Baptist Convention (<www.erlc.com>); the Family Research Council (<www.frc.org>); our own H.O.P.E. Ministries (<www.AboutHope.Org>); and our church (<www.fbcspringdale.org>). We must stay informed, not only about our nation's laws, but concerning the laws of God.

• *Let your voice be heard*

I am personally grateful that, as I write in this season of momentous change, a Bible-reading, praying, and convictional leader occupies the White House. But the greatest need in America is not for a Republican President. It is not for a Democrat Commander-in-Chief. It is not for an Independent in the Oval Office. The greatest need in America is for God to rattle and shake up the Church house to such a degree that it will shake up the state house, reaching all the way to the White House of our nation. Remember that many of our nation's top leaders have heard from the gay lobby MORE than they have from proponents of traditional families. This must change or else . . . we lose America.

It is time now to call the judges and courts of this land back into balance. It is time to sign into law statutes that will confirm what this nation has always believed about marriage and family.

Don't forget that many of our nation's top leaders have heard more from the gay lobby than they have from proponents of traditional families. Let's make sure that in the future, the Speaker of the U. S. House of Representatives can never again say that he hasn't heard much from Christians.

• *Make sure your brand of Christianity has something great to offer*

Cultural extremism takes many forms, but when it comes to Christianity, few are willing to be extreme, to be radical, to stand up and pay the price. Few Christians in this culture live with a faith hot for God, convinced they must become all that God wants them to be, regardless of the consequences.

I'm not talking about being obnoxious. I'm not talking about being offensive. I'm talking about making truth and love our constant, spiritual companions.

Every day, many people drive by a church and have no clue what it is. In fact, most don't *care* who we are. They see us on television and flip the channel. Why aren't they interested? *Because they don't see that Christianity is worth living.* Make sure that when they look at you, they see something in your faith worth having.

Gays and lesbians were — some of them — rejected by the Church when they were beginning to ask questions about their sexuality. Where was our love, understanding, and assistance? They left the people where they should have discovered truth wrapped in acceptance and love, leaving for a cynical people who met them with opened arms, error, and embracement. What a tragedy.

The Church lost our biblical footing . . . our authority, I might add . . . our only authority. The result was that the Word of God, the Bible, became mocked and ignored, becoming just another book in the eyes of our culture. Well, it is more than just another book. It is our authority for life, faith, and practice. It is our light and our truth, and provides our way. Why? It is simple. Not because it is the book of the year . . . don't sell it that short, friend — it is the Book of the Ages!

What We Have Learned — What We Can Do

The Top Ten Things We've Learned

My goal is for you to understand and apply several things this book presents. Processing information, combined with prayer and action, will have a positive impact on our culture. These points will arm you with basic information in answering the Gay Agenda.

Point #1: The Bible's authority has been attacked for a very long time.

Liberal scholars, seminary professors, and even media types have made a mockery of the Bible's history and philosophy for many decades. Christians especially have been intimidated into silence, assuming that these blasphemous attacks will be answered by someone else. Learn to challenge nonsensical assertions, such as "Paul was a repressed gay man." Ask proponents of this view to cite biblical and extra-biblical evidence to prove this kind of point.

Point #2: In recent elections, Christians don't fully participate.

This enables liberal agendas to become the law of the land. Leading Christian figures like Charles Colson, James Dobson, Don Wildmon, James Kennedy, and Jerry Falwell are issuing a clarion call for Christians to become engaged in cultural debate and the shaping of our courts and political offices. I join these giants in asking you to engage in this culture debate and war. Congressional leaders *will* respond to those who contact them, their constituents.

Point #3: Liberal sources are attempting to re-define human sexuality.

After attacking the Bible (our only source for true living), proponents of the Gay Agenda tell us that not only homosexuality, but "trans-gender," bi-sexuality, and beyond are acceptable in a tolerant society. It has been pointed out correctly that what we have always understood as legitimate sex — that between a married man and his wife — can now be expanded to include multiple sex partners of the same gender. Even the abomination of adult sex with under-age children is being legitimized in certain (expanding) circles.

Point #4: Adam and Eve are no myth.

The biblical history tells us, the Word himself tells us, that in the beginning, male and female were made. The fourth chapter of Genesis tells us that Adam knew his wife, not his brother, or some animal. The Bible is our model for all things, including relationships between men and women.

Point #5: Influencing our courts begins with knowledge and prayer.

Our judicial system, from the U.S. Supreme Court all the way to the smallest municipal courts, are made up of interpreters of feelings and liberal agendas, not interpreters of the U.S. Constitution. Our justices on the Supreme Court are imposing their own world views on decisions that affect the entire nation. Justice Anthony Kennedy, and judges in the current "battleground states" struggling with gay issues, are quite open about their interpretations.

Point #6: Don't assume that politicians will "do the right thing" automatically.

The president has endorsed the idea of an amendment to the Constitution, sealing the definition of marriage as "one man for one woman." Sadly, congressional leaders have stated that they are not hearing from Christians and other social conservatives regarding this issue. Although polls clearly indicate that two-thirds of Americans are opposed to same-sex marriage, those views are not being heard in Washington D.C., while the gay lobby is networked, motivated, and aggressive in their lobby efforts.

Point #7: Engagement in the voting process is a duty and freedom.

Recent elections tell us that only a small minority of conservative, family-oriented Christians make an effort to vote on all levels.

This is a major reason that enemies of traditional families have taken the White House and both branches of Congress in the past. These politicians who hold high office are not shy about networking with the gay lobby, in an attempt to be "inclusive" and tolerant. This strategy is helping them get elected, which enables them to implement policies that undermine the American family.

Point #8: "Moral relativism" has crept into our culture in a big way.

Whether it's in a university class, or through the entertainment culture, the view that truth is up to the individual has become pervasive in America today. When truth is relative, it means that right and wrong are never something we can be sure of, but rather depend on shifting feelings and circumstances. This is rigidly opposed to the Bible, which tells us that Jesus Christ is truth.

Point #9: Liberals count on the "niceness" of Christians in changing culture.

Inherent in authentic Christianity is a desire for justice, peace-making, and compassion. Those are certainly hallmarks of Scripture, but they go along with and complement the biblical injunction to "contend earnestly for the faith," and to stand for truth. We can do both if we commit to uphold God's love with one hand, and His truth in the other. This can be done and must be done, in order to confront the Gay Agenda in a balanced way.

Point #10: Homosexuals and Heterosexuals alike need Jesus Christ.

No matter who we are, or where we are, the human need is for a relationship with the true God, Jesus Christ. Jesus alone heals our pain and sin, and in fact promises to do so (Matt. 28). Those trapped in the gay lifestyle, such as Stephen Bennett, have found the way to glorious freedom. Forgiveness of sin and freedom to fully live out one's destiny is available from the only One who can heal. The Church of Jesus Christ today needs to promote that "agenda" and commit to doing so in a more dramatic way than we've seen to date.

The Top 10 Actions We Must Take

If we want to see a cultural revolution in America concerning the present views on homosexuality and the aggressive actions of the gay agenda, then we must act. Yes, based upon what we have learned, I am compelled to call you to take these actions. Not next year . . . not when you get around to it . . . but today. Urgency must become our passion.

Action #1: Renew our commitment to biblical authority and fidelity.

Until we come back to believing in the authority and infallibility of Holy Scripture, we will continue in the shifting cultural sands that are drowning us. Since the Bible is authoritative, we cannot be soft on any sin, including the sin of homesexuality.

God never tolerates it. The Bible calls us to faithfulness in all of its teachings. The Gay lifestyle is a violation of biblical authority, indicating infidelity to Scripture and God.

Action #2: Revive The Church of Jesus Christ.

The sleeping, passive Church of America and the world must wake up. A preacher or politician cannot wake up the Church. Only a great moving of God in our nation will wake up the church of Jesus Christ. We must pray for a mighty moving of God to change our direction or else we will continue to be blown by the strong left winds of our culture. Oh God, revive Your church!

Action #3: Reform our understanding of Human Sexuality.

Sexuality is not and cannot be genderless. God created male and female. We must ignore and destroy any attempt to feminize the masculine or masculinize the feminine. While unisex might exist with sunglasses, it does not ever exist in reality. There is no need to recreate a new understanding of human sexualty; just return to what God has stated it was in the beginning.

Action #4: Refresh our Commitment to Authentic Marriage.

Authentic marriage is marriage between a man and a woman. The term "same-sex marriage" is an oxymoron. If it is not marriage in God's eyes, it is not marriage. The only marriage is between one man and one woman. Remember, it was Adam and Eve, not Adam and Steve.

Action #5: Redesign the Judicial System in our Nation.

The judicial system in our land is in need of a major redesign in function and appearance. The function is now leaning out of balance toward human interpretation or preference. The appearance is completely out of balance. It is time to return to the law — real law — based off of God's Word. It has been stated that the next president of the United States may have the responsibility to appoint three persons to the United States Supreme Court. We had better be asking, "What authority do these candidates live by and what is their commitment to life and marriage?"

Action #6: Remind the Politicians of What We Believe.

Silence cannot be tolerated any longer by those of us who believe in authentic marriage. The politicians of our nation must hear from you. Do not assume they believe the way you do or they do not care what you think. They will listen to the people who e-mail, call, write, or give to them. Please notify your politician right now of your opposition to gay marriage and your support of authentic marriage.

Action #7: Register to Vote and Then Vote!

Are you registered to vote? If not, register today. If you are registered to vote, then vote! Every election is very important. You cannot stay home . . . trust the other guy to represent you . . .

not believe your vote does not count. Remember the presidential election of 2000 — remember Florida? In your church and in other entities, have voter registration efforts where people can register right there in that setting. Encourage . . . encourage . . . and yes, *encourage people to vote!*

Action #8: Reconnect With Morality

Morality is not determined by the "user" or the "moment." Morality occurs by our conscience that originally was pure and right. It is only by sin and evil that our conscience becomes warped and calloused. Morality is not a matter of interpretation. It is a matter of authority. The authority is never "our view," but it is always God's Word — the Bible.

Action #9: Rekindle the Fire to Fight in our Culture.

Our fight is not against flesh and blood, but Satan and his degenerate, degrading ways. His powerful demonic force has blinded the eyes of our generation, leading the culture into deceitful practices especially regarding sexuality. It is time to fight! Not physically, but aggressively by standing up for authentic marriage and for what is right. If you do not fight, your children and grandchildren will be raised in a gay-driven culture that will turn into a gay-led culture in the educational, legal, moral, political, and religious worlds. In other words, if we do not fight the fight, we will lose our culture. Go with God's Word in the power of God's Spirit and fight the fight!!!

Action #10: Respond to Jesus Christ

Religion or law offers no offer. Our hope must be in a personal relationship with Jesus Christ. Jesus died for the sins of the world. Jesus died for you and me, regardless of where we have been, where we are, and where we are going. Ask Jesus Christ to come into your life right now. Ask Him to forgive you of all of your sins, and surrender your life to Him. When you do this right where you are right now, Christ will come into your life, take away your sins, and give you the promise of heaven when you die. It all begins with responding to Jesus Christ. I have never known one person who has given their life to Christ that ever regretted doing so. Respond to Jesus Christ and I guarantee you will begin to see everything, including authentic marriage and human sexuality, in the way that God sees them. Just bow your head right now and respond to Jesus Christ.

SEAL UP THE DIVISIONS

The starter's gun has sounded, the gay lobby is sprinting toward the finish line — and too many of us are still down in the blocks.

Who will win? Who will become the conscience of America? Unless we get busy, friends, it won't be us.

An active member of a church suddenly stopped attending services. The pastor noticed and decided to visit this wayward member of his congregation.

When he arrived at the man's house, the man invited him to come in and sit by the fire. Neither spoke; both knew the reason for the visit, and both felt a bit uncomfortable.

After a time, the pastor stood in front of the fire. He took some iron tongs, pulled a glowing ember from the fire, and placed it by itself on the hearth. He looked at it for a long time, which puzzled his host. Soon the bewildered man began to stare, too.

In time, the pastor once more took the tongs and picked up the darkened coal. Carefully he placed it back into the fire — and in moments it came to life, glowing and white-hot.

The pastor put down the tongs and headed for the door. As he exited, his host said, "Pastor, thanks for the fiery sermon you just preached me. I'll see you in church Sunday."

Our lives must light a path that warms the hearts of all around us. It's true that the Gay Agenda has rocked us. Now it's time for us to get engaged with resolute and fearless spirits. The secret to real happiness, whether for a middle-aged truck driver or a young gay man in New York City, is life in Jesus Christ. We must show them His love. We must love men, women, and children into the Kingdom, just like Jesus did.

So let us seal up the divisions. The truth trumpet is sounding in our ears. We've been apart too long.

I'll see you in church this Sunday.

ENDNOTES

Introduction
1. Charles Colson, address at Mega-Metro Conference for Senior Pastors, Naples, FL, April 20, 2004.

Chapter 1
1. From the pamphlet *Homosexuals: Victims of the Nazis, 1933–45* (Washington D.C.: United States Holocaust Memorial Museum).
2. Judy Shepard, "Five Years Later, Progress Against Gay Hatred Lags," *USA Today* (Oct. 12, 2003).
3. Erik Nelson, "UM Seminary Official Promotes Homosexuality to Youth," *UMAction* (June 7, 2001).
4. Rev. Barbara Cawthorne Crafton, "Can You Believe It?" The Protestant Hour, June 2, 1996, <http://www.prtvc.org>.
5. Ibid.
6. Charles Krauthammer, "When John and Jim Say 'I Do.' " *Time* magazine (July 22, 1996).
7. Bob Stith, "Freedom in Christ," *For Faith and Family's Light* magazine (Sept./Oct. 2003): p. 5.

Chapter 2
1. Jeffrey Ressner, "10 Questions for Oliver Stone," *Time* magazine (April 19, 2004).
2. Larry King, interview with Dr. James Dobson, "Larry King Live," Sept. 5, 2003.
3. Supreme Court of the United States Syllabus, *Lawrence et al. v. Texas*, Certiorari to the Court of Appeals of Texas, Fourteenth District, No. 02–102; argued March 26, 2003, decided June 26, 2003.
4. CNN.com, Oct. 28, 2003.
5. *National Liberty Journal* (May 12, 2000).
6. *AFA Journal* (June 1997): p. 7.
7. Albert Mohler, "Television's Fall Schedule: The Homosexual Agenda Advances," Crosswalk.com.
8. Robert Tanner, Associated Press, March 5, 2004.
9. The Pew Forum on Religion and Public Life, "Republicans Unifed, Democrats Split on Gay Marriage," online.
10. Ibid.
11. The Associated Press, "Methodists Propose Formal Split Over Gays," May 7, 2004.
12. "The Verdict That Shook United Methodism" *Good News* magazine (May/June, 1998): p. 12.

Chapter 3

1. Barbara Grady, "Gay Journalists Off California Story After They Marry," Reuters, March 15, 2004.
2. News in Brief, "Names and Faces," Arkansas Democrat-Gazette Press Services, April 26, 2004.
3. Ed Vitagliano, "Disney Execs in Collusion With Homosexual Rights Activists," *AFA Journal* (June 1997).
4. American Family Association, "Mainstream Media Applaud Showtime's Perversion," press release, Dec. 8, 2000.
5. GLAAD website, Resource Kits: "Marriage Equality for Same-Sex Couples," May 14, 2004.
6. Action Alert, "Marrriage Protection Week," American Humanist Association website, <http://www.americanhumanist.org/press/actionalerts/aaprotectmarriage.html>.
7. "Time 100: Heroes and Icons," *Time* magazine (April 26, 2004).
8. Evan Wolfson, "Why Are the Polls on 'Gay Marriage' So Inconsistent?" Freedom to Marry website, April 16, 2004.
9. ACLU Fact Sheet, "Overview of Lesbian and Gay Parenting, Adoption and Foster Care, April 6, 1999, <http://archive.aclu.org/issues/gay/parent.html.
10. "Poll: America's Evangelicals More and More Mainstream But Insecure," *Religion & Ethics Newsweekly*, April 13, 2004, <http://www.pbs.org/wnet/religionandethics/week733/release.html.
11. Paul Varnell, "Homosexuality in Leviticus," *Chicago Free Press*, Feb. 4, 2004.
12. James C. Dobson, "Family News from Dr. James Dobson," Focus on the Family, Colorado Springs, CO, April 2004.

Chapter 4

1. Art Moore, "City Ties 'Family Values' to 'Homophobia,'" WorldNetDaily.com, July 31, 2003.
2. "Federal Marriage Amendment Dead?" WorldNetDaily.com, April 20, 2004.
3. President George W. Bush, "President Calls for Constitutional Amendment to Protect Marriage," <http://www.whitehouse.gove/news/releases/2004/02/10040224-2.html>.
4. Supreme Court of the United States Syllabus, *Lawrence et al. v. Texas*, Certiorari to the Court of Appeals of Texas, Fourteenth District, No. 02–102; argued March 26, 2003, decided June 26, 2003.
5. Ibid.
6. Ibid.
7. Ibid.

8. Ibid.
9. Ibid.
10. Ibid.
11. Stephen Dinan, "Backers of Amendment against Same-Sex Union See Texas Ruling as Boost," *Washington Times,* July 7, 2003.
12. Edwin Chen, "Bush Seeks Constitutional Ban on Same-Sex Marriage," *Los Angeles Times*, Feb. 25, 2004.
13. Michael Gormley, "Spitzer: Gay Marriage Illegal in NY," *New York Daily News*, April 3, 2004.
14. Robert Tanner, "State Ags Come Down Against Gay Marriage," KansasCity.com, March 5, 2004.
15. James C. Dobson, "Family News from Dr. James Dobson," Focus on the Family, Colorado Springs, CO, April, 2004.

Chapter 5
1. "Woman Corners Kerry on Issue of Civil Rights, 'Gay Rights,' " *Baptist Press News,* March 7, 2004.
2. Ibid.
3. Ibid.
4. Christopher Hitchens, "Unsafe on Any Ballot," *Vanity Fair* (May 2004): p. 118.
5. "Kerry: Federal Government Should Recognize State-sanctioned Same-Sex 'Marriage,' " *Baptist Press News*, March 4, 2004.
6. Ibid.
7. Michael Slackman, "Same-Sex Marriage Blurs Lines on Both Sides of the Political Aisle," *New York Times*, March 7, 2004.
8. Michael Foust, "Same-Sex 'Marriage': Is There a Republican-Democratic Split?" *Baptist Press News*, April 8, 2004.
9. Ibid.
10. Ibid.
11. The O'Reilly Factor, FOXNews, March 5, 2004.
12. "Defiance, Rebuke on Gay Marriage," Boston.com, May 12, 2004.
13. Ibid.

Chapter 6
1. Tony Campolo, *20 Hot Potatoes Christians Are Afraid To Touch* (Dallas, TX: Word, 1988), p. 109.
2. *Northwest Arkansas Times*, August 17, 2003.
3. Paul Varnell, "Homosexuality in Leviticus," *Chicago Free Press*, Feb. 4, 2004.
4. William Willimon, "Under Fire," *The Christian Century* (May 2, 2001).

5. John Shelby Spong, *Here I Stand* (New York: Harper SanFrancisco, 2000), p. 363.
6. Bob Stith, "Freedom in Christ," *For Faith and Family's Light* magazine (Sept./Oct. 2003): p. 5.
7. Open letter from William Sloane Coffin to Reggie White, *Appleton Post-Crescent*, March 29, 1998.
8. Virginia Ramey Mollenkott, *Omnigender* (Cleveland, OH: Pilgrim Press, 2001), p. 108.
9. Dennis Prager, "Who Supports Same-Sex Marriage?" Townhall. com, March 9, 2004.
10. Russell D. Moore, "Revivalism, Civil Rights, and Same-Sex 'Marriage,' " *SBC Life* (May 2004).
11. Ibid.

Chapter 7

1. Malcom Muggeridge, The End of Christendom (Grand Rapids, MI: Wm. B. Eerdmans, 1980).
2. Kerby Anderson, "The Decline of a Nation," Probe Ministries, <http://www.probe.org/docs/decline.html>.
3. Ibid.
4. "French Socialists Support Marriage Equality," *The Data Lounge* (May 14, 2004).
5. J. Lam, "The Human Rights Court Award Parental Rights to a Gay Man," *TOA* (April 2001).
6. Ibid.
7. "Dockery: Christians Must Not Ignore Cultural Controversies," *Baptist Press News*, May 12, 2004.
8. Kerby Anderson, "The Decline of a Nation," Probe Ministries, <http://www.probe.org/docs/decline.html>.
9. CNN.com, "Anti-gay Marriage Act Clears Congress," Sept. 10, 1996.
10. Ibid.
11. "Pope: Same-Sex Unions 'Degrade' Marriage," *USA Today* (Feb. 28, 2004).
12. Dr. Ira Gallaway, "Tears of Grief and Sorrow," *We Confess* (March/April 2004).
13. Coral Ridge Ministries news release, "D. James Kennedy Applauds President Bush for Announcing Support for Federal Marriage Amendment," Feb. 24, 2004.
14. Allison Schlesinger, "Pennsylvania Presbyterian Church Cuts Ties with 10 Presbyteries," Boston.com, April 27, 2004.
15. "Gay Bishop Loses License After Marrying," *The Data Lounge* (May 10, 2004).